SELF-MASTERY AND FATE
WITH THE CYCLES OF LIFE

∇   ∇   ∇

Self-Mastery and Fate

With the Cycles of Life

by
H. Spencer Lewis

Published by the Grand Lodge of the
English Language Jurisdiction, AMORC, Inc.
1342 Naglee Avenue, San Jose, CA 95191
www.rosicrucian.org

DEDICATION

Δ

TO THE GLORY OF THE MODERN MEN AND WOMEN

who are sufficiently broad in their thinking
to adopt new methods to achieve
success and happiness,
THIS BOOK IS DEDICATED
that it may be a token of the first
step in their lives, leading to
SELF-MASTERY

Δ

CONTENTS

THE LAW OF PERIODICITY

Δ

"There is a tide in the affairs of men, which, taken at the flood, leads on to fortune."

—Shakespeare

"To every thing there is a season, and a time to every purpose under the heaven: A time to be born, and a time to die; a time to plant, and a time to pluck up that which is planted."

—King Solomon

INTRODUCTION

It is a pleasure to say a few words to the readers of this book and perhaps prepare them for the great treat that is in store for them.

The system presented in the following pages is so unique, so startling, and yet so surprisingly useful in a very dependable way that I feel that each reader will want to know a little about the origin of the system and its past use.

Those who have read the author's helpful book entitled *Rosicrucian Principles for the Home and Business* will recall that practically every page of that book identified Dr. Lewis with the intimate, inner activities of many large corporations and business organizations. In fact, that book revealed the secret of the former lifework of Dr. Lewis before he left the business field and devoted himself almost exclusively to the direction of the affairs of the Rosicrucian Order in North America. Those of us who were acquainted with him and who are familiar with his past life readily understand what was meant when Arthur Stillwell, the former president of many financial institutions and one of the foremost builders of railroads in America, said: "H. Spencer Lewis has been the real 'silent partner' and secret adviser in more big business propositions in America than any other living man."

Even to this very day [1929] with his many activities in connection with the Rosicrucian Order, he is consulted by long-distance telephone from all parts of America, and by telegrams and letters from boards of directors and presidents of corporations, asking for one of his strange and always dependable decisions in regard to some contemplated action or some problem that presents two phases, two solutions, or two possible lines of action.

For over twenty years the question has been asked thousands of times by as many business men, "What peculiar system or method does this man use which enables him to tell us what we should do or what we should not do, and *when* and *how* we should proceed in our business affairs?" It was not a purely selfish motive that caused Dr. Lewis to keep to himself, in this country, the secret of his system, and use it to help those who consulted him. While large fees have been paid to him for his services—and even today he is the recipient of shares of interests unanimously voted to him by corporations, boards of directors, and individuals as a result of his definite assistance in crucial times—I have known of hundreds of instances wherein he had gladly and wholeheartedly given his advice and help without fee, and without any prospect of remuneration of any kind. But the use of this system was his business and he had neither the time nor the inclination to establish a school or private class for the teaching and impartation of his system to others.

The time has come, however, when he feels that his services to the organization should occupy most of his time, and that his interests in other big business propositions are sufficiently varied and successful to require no additions thereto. Therefore, he has decided to relinquish his system and give it to the world in such form that every man and every woman, young or old, in business or out of business, may use some part of it to bring greater success, prosperity, and happiness into their lives.

And so the system has been reduced to words, charts, and diagrams. I marveled at the fundamental explanations contained in the first few chapters of his manuscript. What a world of simplicity is revealed in the cosmic laws manifesting through the strange cycles of vibrations! The first few chapters are worthy of a book printed in gold and bound in rarest metals. These alone would bring to any business man or woman the necessary *key* for the understanding of the peculiar fluctuations, changes, and unexpected occurrences that arise in all personal and business affairs, and that bring problems, trials, and tribulations of grave concern. To know why these things occur, and that there is a periodicity to them and that they are not by mere chance or coincidence, is to remove them from the category of the *unknowable* which torments the life and soul of every business man and woman.

The chapters which follow, and which reveal the fact that man as a free agent can become the master of his fate and the director of his destiny, are chapters that will become a monument to the many marvelous contributions this author has made to human welfare. The words in these chapters will become the agency for the breaking of the chains and fetters which have enslaved thousands of persons and held them in the bondage of miscomprehension regarding the events of their lives and the possibilities that lie dormant within their own beings.

To have all of this followed by the many chapters that explain in detail the various cycles and periods of conditions which affect our personal and business affairs, our health, our pleasures, our hopes, and ambitions, is to have added to the priceless treasury of the early chapters a veritable casket of rare jewels. As I tested the cycles and the periodical effects in a review of my own life for the past ten years, I saw before me a map of all that I had passed through and a well-charted survey of what I *might* have accomplished, what I *might* have attained, and what I *might* have brought into my own life if I had used this system years ago. I saw, too, in the charts that I had made roughly, with no difficulty and with intense pleasure, a complete outline of what I can accomplish next month, next year, and for many years in the future; and I saw my course through life charted now as clearly as a ship charts its course across the sea when it proceeds from the shores and heads its bow toward the seemingly unknown space beyond.

One word of warning would I give to every reader of this book: Read carefully every word of the first chapters of this book, digesting every thought and principle, and become well acquainted with each idea that is successively presented in the paragraphs that fill its chapters. It is only through understanding the principles before applying the cycles to our own intimate affairs that anyone can reap the greatest good out of this remarkable manuscript.

The years will come and go, and many more unusual, fascinating, and helpful contributions will be made to the mystical, metaphysical, and psychological literature of America, but there never will be another book or another manuscript that will prove as revolutionary, as astounding, and as unique in its practical information as this book now before you. It will do more to rob superstitious beliefs regarding cosmic influences of their enslaving hold on the minds of many and to bring to man a realization of his greatest assets and powers than anything that has been published since the dawn of civilization. It will become a high testimonial to the rare knowledge possessed by a Rosicrucian and to the high character, motives and ideals, and activities of those who are devoting their lives unselfishly through the Rosicrucian Order to the benefit of all mankind.

E. V. R.—1929

SELF-MASTERY AND FATE

CHAPTER 1

THE PROBLEM OF MASTERSHIP

M AN is either a victim of fate or the master of his destiny! There are no two ways about it, and no neutral position. I am speaking, of course, of mankind and not of the individual. There are individuals who are masters and creators of their destinies part of their lives, and innocent or despondent victims of fate at other times. The lives of such persons simply prove the fact that man can be master or slave as he chooses.

The system set forth in this book for the attainment and application of self-mastership, or the mastership over so-called fatalistic conditions, is based upon the premise that man is essentially a creator of his environment and his circumstances, and not the result of these things. Usually a premise is an assumption or a supposition, but I trust that my readers will see before they have completed the reading of this book that the premise in this case is a fact, and that the other facts in the system built upon this premise substantiate and demonstrate the fundamental fact.

Therefore, if you are one of the many who have been led to believe that environment has gradually molded civilization, and that it has specifically made of man what he is and still controls him, I implore you for your own sake and your own best interests to lay aside that belief and, for the time of the reading of this book and the testing of its principles, to assume the premise upon which this system is founded to be true and thereby give it every opportunity to serve you.

The fundamental principle involved in this system of self-mastery is that which was observed centuries ago by those untutored and nonacademic minds which had to depend upon the casual and multifarious manifestations of man's existence and nature's operations to determine the natural laws in both the spiritual and material kingdoms. That principle, evolved through observation and perfected through test and application, reveals that all life and all existence within the universe has its expression in cycles, the periodicity of which is equivalent to the rhythm of certain measured and harmonious recurrences of stresses or impulses of a cosmic nature.

Modern science in its laboratory examination of the microscopical manifestations of natural law has discovered that all cells of living matter, and all crystals of nonliving matter, have varying periods of rhythmic motion beginning with their birth and controlling the process of development to maturity, and guiding the evolutionary steps preceding the process of breaking down or reproducing others of their own species. And it has been found that the periodicity which distinguishes the rhythm of each of these species or classifications of matter is harmoniously related to the periodicity observable in the movements of the planets and the effects of rhythm on the tides of the waters of the Earth, and the growth of plant life as well as animal life.

Even in the functioning of the organs of animal bodies—such as the breathing processes, the heart action, and similar movements contributing to the maintenance of life—

there is a definite rhythm closely resembling, and having a harmonic relation to, the larger and more pronounced rhythms of the cosmic energy.

It is not my intention to be highly technical nor even academic in my explanation of the laws and principles pertaining to the cause of the universal rhythm which constitutes the motion of life. Such facts are contained in the Rosicrucian teachings for those who are devoting their lives to the profound research work in which Rosicrucian scientists have been eminent for many centuries. Suffice it to say that there are certain self-evident facts, and others easily demonstrable, which supply the basis for further study in this direction.

It is my intention to speak specifically in this book of the rhythm of life as it affects man and his interests. Even a casual study of the system represented in this book will open the doorway to such mastership of the practical affairs of our daily lives that there will be no room left, in the minds of any who test the system, for doubt as to the universality of the law involved and its universal effect upon all life and all things seemingly without life.

The question has often been discussed as to whether man is a free agent or not, and a test of the system contained in this book will reveal to anyone that, insofar as having the right and privilege to choose is concerned, man is absolutely a free agent. But, he will also find that not a personal God but an impersonal cosmic law holds him responsible for his choice in each and every instance.

We see throughout our lives the success of those men and women who seem to have been fortunate in their choice of professions, occupations, or applications of time, or who were "lucky" in their selection of property, material, place, or time for the attainment of wealth and happiness, or who followed continuously some intuitive urges which actuated them in their affairs at most propitious times. We see, on the other hand, those who seem to be most unfortunate in all of these things; and, in ignorance of the laws involved, we may be apt to attribute the fortunes and misfortunes to chance or to fate.

It is the purpose of the system set forth in this book to enable every man, woman, and child to take advantage of certain natural laws and work in harmony with them to the end that each may be master of his fate, and, through harmonious cooperation with the cycles of life, reap the richest rewards offered by the bountiful disposition of the cosmic plan.

Without resort, therefore, to superstitious beliefs or practices, and without invoking the questionable influence of hypothetical and theoretical powers of an invisible nature, and with all the saneness and rationalism of a scientific method of living, the practical men and women of this modern time—even those who may be prejudiced against that which is unique or metaphysical—may bring large and important changes into their lives and redirect the courses of their careers toward a certain and assured goal.

With such a desire in mind, let the reader analyze carefully the brief explanations of the laws and principles which follow in the succeeding chapters, without slighting one of them and without minimizing their importance because of their simplicity.

CHAPTER 2

MAN A FREE AGENT

IN considering man's actions as free or controlled, or as controllable or destined, the important point to be examined is this: Are our acts the result of antecedent causes, or are we directed in all of our affairs by external influences, such as the so-called cosmic vibrations, mental impulses from without, or tendencies in and around us? In other words, are our lives as we live them generally an effect of our environment and invisible impulses and urges over which we have no control, and by which certain opportunities and temptations are brought before us and which we either accept and utilize or deny and cast aside?

Those who argue that man is a free agent, and is not governed by any external influences, are begging the question and reaching no conclusion whatsoever. Man is a free agent in every sense that the most enthusiastic of the exponents of that doctrine would have us believe; but that means that man is ever free to choose, to select, elect, and determine what he wills to do in each and every circumstance. It implies that man is never forced against his will to do anything or even think anything.

Of course, the real intent of the doctrine of free agency as promulgated by many schools of philosophical thought is to decry the fact that man is affected in any way by the wishes of God, the autocracy of natural and spiritual law, and the inevitable workings of heredity. These things, however, do not affect man in the sense usually presented by these philosophical schools, or by the fanatics who misunderstand the real principles.

The wishes of God may truly be the dictates of an omnipotent being, and man is unquestionably affected by the will of God. The method whereby the will and desires of God are expressed and brought to the consciousness of man, however, is little understood even by those who devote their lives to the propounding of God's laws and His direction of the universe. The belief in a personal God who has destined and decreed for each individual before birth a course and a career which will inevitably become manifest in the life of each individual after birth, regardless of the will of man and his application of the divine power within him, which is his birthright, is a pagan belief, unsupported by the testimonies of life itself and by the revelations of spiritual and natural law when applied understandingly.

Students may learn, through the present system, that the will and wishes of God are expressed to man in the form of inspirations, and these inspirations may be carried to man through tendencies, impulses, urges, and propitious presentations in the form of opportunities and temptations. And, man is as often *tempted* to do good as to do evil. The same may be said of any of the true principles of planetary or other cosmic influences. In each case their effect upon man is in the form of these tendencies, without the power to enforce their acceptance by man. Therefore, we find that man is continuously and constantly affected by the opportune temptations to act or to think. Merciful indeed, and just, was God in giving to man the power and the privilege to choose and to decide for himself when he finds himself tempted by opportunities, urged by inspiration, or led by impulses. And—as a free agent to choose between one impulse and another, one inspiration and another, or one temptation and another—he must abide by his decision and assume the responsibility.

Agreeing, therefore, that man is a free agent and has the privilege and power to choose in all of his acts and in all of his thinking, we still have to consider the nature and the source of these impulses, urges, and inspirations that come before him, and which call for a choice or a choosing. If there were not diverse opportunities presenting themselves, and if there were not varying impulses, urges, and inspirations occurring momentarily, hourly, daily throughout the life of man, there would be no reason for man to have the ability and the power to choose, and man would not have been given the ability to reason, to think, and to use his will power.

The unconscious machinery of the factory has neither the ability to analyze nor the power to act as a free agent. Of all living things, man is unique in that he possesses to the highest degree the ability to act freely and to choose of his own volition. And it may be no tribute to mankind in general to say that the majority has chosen most often unwisely, and that to the minority has been left the salvation and advancement of the race through the proper exercise of its great prerogative.

In the year 1918 I wrote a monograph on this subject, and I stated therein that this subject of impulses, inspirations, and tendencies continuously presented to man for his choice "in conjunction with the study of the law of compensation, is worthy of a complete book which I may prepare if I find a demand for it." I believe that the time has come for man, in the Occidental world, to know more about these laws and to live in harmony with them as have the Masters of the Far East, and the highly developed and successful persons of the Orient.

The business man is constantly confronted, in the affairs of his daily life, with the necessity of deciding between two plans, two urges, two propositions, two temptations, two "hunches." Or, there may be several distinctly different impulses and plans before him calling for a choice. He is also confronted with the diverse tendencies of his affairs to choose between a greater development of some of them, or a curtailment of others. He is confronted yearly with the problem of expansion or retraction. He finds himself face to face with important decisions, which must be made, that affect the present and future standing of his business and the success of his personal or business career.

The woman in the home finds herself facing similar problems. From day to day there are two urges, impulses, and temptations presented by the affairs of the members of her family, the arguments of solicitors and salesmen, the perplexities of her husband's personal affairs which bear upon the growth and development of the family and its best interests, and her own personal and intimate affairs. The woman in business and the young man in business just starting their careers, or trying to establish themselves in a selected field of effort, find themselves continuously called upon in the quiet of their personal examinations to make decisions that will unquestionably affect the remainder of their lives. To them, as to all others, come the urges and impulses, the opportunities and temptations, the desires and wishes, with both negative and positive phases to be considered, and a choice to be decided upon.

As these persons decide, so will they determine their *fates* and establish their destinies. The fate of a day, like the fate of a year, may leave its fortunate or unfortunate results to affect the entire life and career of a person or a business.

Yielding to an urge or an inspiration, or submitting to an impulse or temptation, or taking advantage of an opportunity with no other warrant or reason than the judgment based upon analytical reasoning, is equivalent in most cases to choosing between right and wrong by the toss of a coin. Man's reasoning cannot rise higher than the premises upon which it is based, and the premises of knowledge forming the foundation of man's analytical reasoning may be faulty because they may not include a knowledge of the external influences and the natural laws governing his life and his affairs.

As the system contained in this book will show, there is a periodicity or cycle of periods regulating unfortunate periods in the life of each being, also the movement, progression, development, and maturity of each thing in life which begins at a point and proceeds onward to a conclusion—whether that thing is a business proposition, a journey, the building of a house or factory, the buying and selling of merchandise, the diseases and illnesses of the flesh, the conception and development of an embryo, the movement of the tides, or anything that is created and brought into existence by natural laws through divine decree or man's volition.

By working in harmony with the periods of one's own personal life and the periods of the business plan, proposition, or creation of man's thinking, the utmost success will be made and attained, while working out of harmony with these periods or in ignorance of them will bring frustration, failure, losses, and defeat.

Man is the free agent to choose whether he will work in harmony with the universal law of rhythm, whether he will choose rightly or wrongly. But the result of his choice will automatically follow, and this inevitable result constitutes a manifestation of the law of compensation.

He who chooses rightly and works in harmony with the law becomes the master of his fate, while he who fails to choose rightly and works out of harmony with the law is a slave to fate and a victim of destiny unconsciously created.

CHAPTER 3

COSMIC RHYTHM AND THE CYCLES OF LIFE

THE foolish person tries to ignore the phenomenal facts of life simply because he cannot learn the logical theory which explains them. With all the logic at our command, we may reason out of the domain of possibilities everything that may be called a theoretical explanation of the cosmic rhythm which produces the various cycles of life, but we cannot with the same logic and reasonableness negate the facts which have been observed. To the same degree that one may claim that electricity does not exist because its source and its nature may not be known to everyone who reads—yet by its manifestations it proves to be a fact in the phenomenal world—so we may ignore the invisible vibrations of cosmic rhythm and smile at the possibility of these things being divided into manifest cycles or periods, yet the phenomenal facts are quite observable and undeniable.

There are explanations which scientists may call *theoretical,* and metaphysicians will call *true,* which reveal the laws and principles of cosmic vibrations. But these explanations have no place in this book, and in fact deal with the fundamentals of the secret teachings of the Rosicrucians which may not be set forth in any public book, or printed in any public form. Moreover, these facts would not serve any purpose at this time, and, believing that this book will be perused by those of the practical type of mind who wish a system that is workable, without the need of profound study, I will avoid any unnecessary postulations regarding the laws of the cosmic or spiritual world.

It is sufficient to say, therefore, that all energy in the universe, of whatever nature, has but a single source, but in its emanations and radiations becomes divided into various phases of undulations which the Rosicrucians have called *vibrations*. These undulations have certain periodicity or periods of kinetic and static manifestations, much like the radiations from the antenna of a transmitting radio station. We may think of these various undulations as being of different wavelengths, different rates of vibrations, or different periods as we please, but the fact is that the resulting effects from the different waves or radiations account for the various forms of known and unknown energies in the universe.

I will presume that those interested in the study of vibrations, so-called, realize that vibrations may be divided into a great many octaves of manifestation, and each octave may be divided into many distinct forms of manifestation in both the spiritual and material world. Even the few octaves which cover the manifestation of sound give a wide variation of manifestation; for some of the rates within the octaves of sound may be so low as to be inaudible to the average person, and manifest only through touch, while others may be so high as to be inaudible but manifest in light or other mental or metaphysical ways. Ordinary electricity is unquestionably another form of the periodic range of the universal vibrations, as is the divine essence of the soul, the vital life force of the animal body, and the lower vibrations of vitality in plant and mineral life.

In addition to the above manifestations caused by the varying rates of vibrations of cosmic energy we find that the energy controls and directs the rhythmic motion of all things in the universe, and I hardly need to remind my reader of the fact that motion is the fundamental principle of all material things, and that if motion were eliminated in the universe, we would see, hear, feel, and sense nothing. Matter itself is a result of the motion in the electrons, which is carried into the atoms and molecules. And the electronic motion is a result of the motion impregnated by the rhythmic pulsations of cosmic energy.

As stated in a previous paragraph, everything that is in the universe is existing and manifesting in accordance with a cycle of rhythm distinctly its own, and everything that has had a beginning or a start whereby it became a distinct entity moves forward in time in accordance with a cycle of progression distinctly its own. Those who have had the pleasure of reading the more simple explanations of Einstein's hypothesis of relativity, coupled with other recent, simple explanations of the theoretical relationship of time, motion, and space, will realize that time itself is an artificial relationship between motion and our consciousness and apprehension.

When it was learned that our sight-consciousness required a minimum of one eighth of a second to apprehend an impression, and that the impression registered upon the retina of the eye remained in the consciousness one sixteenth of a second after the sight impression had left the retina, it was found that by having the sight impression last one sixteenth and the consciousness of it remain for one sixteenth, we had an apprehensive period of two sixteenths of a second, or one eighth of a second, divided into one sixteenth of actual physical impression and one sixteenth of retentive impression. This was a discovery made through what might be called experimental psychology, coupled with a truly metaphysical analysis of the time element in conscious apprehension.

Out of this metaphysical or almost mystical analysis evolved the very practical invention of the kinetoscope which was later evolved step by step into the present-day motion-picture camera and projector. It is from the fundamental fact, however, that objective, worldly consciousness requires the element of time to apprehend and translate its apprehension into understanding, that we have become accustomed to associate a definite period of endurance or progression to the existence of all things. And we unconsciously establish a scale or standard of measurement of time whereby we may be conscious, relatively, of the existence of each thing in life.

It is known to the Rosicrucians who taught the principles of relativity and the fundamentals of the hypothetical conditions called *time* and *space*, long before Einstein or his predecessors, that the psychic consciousness of man does not require the element of time in its apprehension which is required by the objective or worldly consciousness, and, therefore, in the dream state or in any psychic state, the progression of facts evolving in the consciousness does not require the element of time for apprehension; the progression or sequence of events is disassociated from the objective standard of measurement of the time element.

Thus, in a dream or in a psychic state of consciousness events may occur and be apprehended by the consciousness in a flash of a second; but, when translated by the objective consciousness in a waking state, require minutes to explain and become associated with a period of time of from five minutes to five hours or more. It is not uncommon for a dream that seemed to cover a relatively objective period of an hour or more, to have actually required a negligible fraction of time to occur in the psychic state. In fact, we have no reason at all to believe that occurrences in the psychic state have any period of the time element in them whatsoever. They do not progress in relation to our objective consciousness of time.

In more simple words we may say that all events and all things existing as eventful are associated by the objective consciousness with time, since they require time to be apprehended by our objective minds. It is a fact that we cannot be conscious in an analytical way of two things at the same time, and that when we are attempting to be conscious or mindful of two things coincidental in objective time, we can only be conscious of them intermittently by having each different impression follow in sequence, giving each its allotted fraction of a second for apprehension.

Thus a man reading a book may walk along the street among many pedestrians. He may be successful in reading understandingly every word on the page, and at the same time avoid collision with others and make the proper progressive steps, side steps, and hesitations necessary to complete his walk. He may think that he is conscious of his walking, and the control of his steps, at the same time he is conscious of his reading, but in truth he is dividing his attentiveness alternately between the words on the page and the steps he is taking.

Such alternation in conscious apprehension or realization may be so rapid as to seem almost coincidental. It is not the progression of events that actually requires the element of conscious time with which we are familiar, but our consciousness of the progression of events, and this is always relative and fictitious, having no foundation in cosmic terms.

The observable progression of events is impressed upon the consciousness in such periods of time as constitute what is known as a definite periodicity or a definite cycle, and as stated heretofore, each and every event begins a cycle of its own through which it progresses to culmination or to a finality. These cycles are called the *rhythm of life* when associated with our own existence as human beings, but more popularly called *cycles of progression* when related to our material affairs.

Thus each human being has a cycle of existence that is divided into identical periods for all beings. The cycle begins at the first breath of life breathed into the nostrils, and lasts for approximately 144 years. Very few complete this cycle of life because of violation of natural laws or inharmonious living. Worldly events have two cycles—the major and the minor. The major cycle is one sun year, or approximately 365 days, while the minor cycle is one sun day, or approximately 24 hours. Other events or affairs in our lives, such as ill-health in the form of diseases, accidents, and fevers, also have cycles varying in length according to the nature of the thing itself, just as the gestation of the human embryo and of other animal embryos has cycles of distinctive lengths, and as seeds in the ground also have germination cycles.

Each cycle is divided into periods of equal length, and each of these periods produces certain definite effects upon the progression of the thing governed by the cycle. What is meant by this will be explained in the next chapter, but here the important point to bear in mind is that just as the breathing under all conditions and the beating of the heart and of the functioning of other organs within the body are rhythmic and in accordance with certain rates of periodicities which have become standard, and an alteration of which plainly indicates to the physician an abnormal condition, so all things in life move rhythmically, and the normal and natural rhythm for each thing in its cycle is in harmony with the cosmic rhythms. When anything has a rhythm that is out of harmony with the cosmic rhythms it is abnormal or subnormal, and therefore in the process of destruction or frustration. It is by being in rhythm with the Cosmic or in tune with the infinite that man may keep his health and his affairs progressing to the highest degree and manifesting abundantly in health, happiness, prosperity, and peace.

Chapter 4

THE PERIODS OF EARTHLY CYCLES

IN the preceding chapter I stated that as the human being is an entity, physically, so each event or each thing created by nature or by man and having a beginning in the physical expression on this earth plane is an entity, having a cycle of existence distinctly its own. This refers even to diseases, or to so-called accidents, for they, too, are the results of man's actions, and therefore created by him, and have a definite worldly starting point and cycle of existence.

Cycles of time for the existence of things are like lines drawn from starting points and continuing for various lengths. And each of these lines is divided into periods or segments, sections or sectors, as you choose to call them, of equal lengths. Each of these sectors constitutes a different manifestation of cosmic urge, impulse, or influence, tending to direct the progress and development of each thing.

The ancient philosophers accepted the eminent philosopher's statement that in the beginning of all creation, God geometrized. It is true that the more we search into the origin and operation of spiritual and natural law, the more we find that the whole scheme of the universe and the incidental scheme of each individual thing in the universe operates and manifests in accordance with the principles of geometry. Thus God is the great Architect and Mathematician, and the very complex map of geometrical motions and designs for the movement and existence of all things is but slowly being comprehended by man. We may never know the origin and general plan of God's entire universe, and we may never know the reason for the mathematical progression of all events. But we can know through observation and through test and trial the effect of these mathematical progressions in our own lives.

I have stated above that each event begins at a starting point, which is the beginning of a line of progression, and this line constitutes its mathematical cycle equivalent to a curved line beginning at the conception and birth of an event, attaining the peak of the curve at its maturity, and declining in its curve to the last point of culmination or finality. The expression "the course of events" is based upon a very ancient and continuous observation of the fact that most events reveal very clearly a definite course of progression. This fact has been considered so little in the business world by the busy materialist that he has overlooked one of the most helpful of all metaphysical principles, and it is the Rosicrucian alone who constantly maps his life and his daily affairs in accordance with the geometrical progression of mathematical operation throughout life. Hence the secret of his success, his power, and his ability to be a real master of his life instead of a victim of so-called fate.

The Rosicrucian begins his studies by a careful digest of the fundamental cycles of life, and learns to become acquainted with the periodicity of all things in the animal, mineral, and vegetable kingdom. He finally becomes acquainted through the studies with his own relationship to the cosmic cycles and those periods wherein he may do the most desirable things at the propitious times. It is this that has gained for the Rosicrucian throughout the many past centuries the title of Master, for he becomes a master of his own life and his own affairs.

We may liken the line that represents the progressive course of events in life to the charted line drawn upon a map which the captain of an ocean steamship tries to follow when he leaves the port of New York expecting to reach the port of Liverpool. That line upon the map may be several thousand miles long, or it may be said to be seven days long. In the latter case, we may say that the cycle of the journey across the ocean, or the progression of the journey, is seven days long and is divided into seven periods, of one day each. The first period of one day begins at the hour and minute that the ship starts from the wharf. The second period of one day begins just twenty-four hours after that, and the other periods follow in the same manner. Hence the journey is a cycle of seven periods and we would say, therefore, that the periodicity of the cycle of the journey is seven days or seven periods.

Each of these days will produce a different effect in the events of the journey. The first day may produce or manifest a rough sea, with wind and storm. The second day may produce a calm sea, with every advantage for progressing rapidly and making up the time lost during the first day. The third day may produce not only a calm sea but warm temperatures, with a favorable wind enabling everyone to enjoy the journey to the utmost, and enabling the ship to make more rapid movement. The fourth day may produce a moderate sea but a strong headwind that will delay the journey, and the other days may produce still different effects.

If the captain and passengers of the boat knew the true periodicity of their journey, they would be prepared for certain events, and instead of being victims of fate, so-called, they would be forewarned and forearmed to be masters in every condition and circumstance.

The journey of life is much like a journey on the sea, and each life begins at a slightly different starting point. Even casual observation revealed long ago that man's life is divided into periods like the days of the ocean journey, with definite events occurring during each period. The average human being is unconscious of these periods, and still more unconscious of any knowledge about the events which are most apt to occur during each of these periods. Therefore, he is unprepared to meet them until they are in full manifestation and is handicapped in solving the problems of life by a lack of knowledge regarding the propitiousness of the tendencies which will be made manifest in each successive period.

The course of a business, whether it be manufacturing, selling merchandise, or some other line of endeavor, has a definite cycle or series of cycles of one year each, beginning with the first day that the business began to operate or the owner or proprietor entered into it. And each of these yearly periods or cycles is divided into segments of definite lengths, wherein certain tendencies, conditions, and circumstances are sure to arise or present themselves, and which may be most unfortunate if unknown or misunderstood, and exceedingly fortunate if appreciated and advantageously accepted.

Thus we see that the cycles of life really constitute a geometrical map or a mathematical scheme whereby we can mechanically and accurately map our lives and the external influences, and either take advantage of these things, or innocently and ignorantly submit to them. In the one case we are masters of our destiny, and in the other case, victims of our fate.

SELF-MASTERY AND FATE

CHAPTER 5

THE SIMPLE PERIODS
OF HUMAN LIFE

———————

ONE of the most simple and very apparent cycles of human life is one which the ancients observed and quickly learned to use as a basis for many of their mathematical and geometrical plans of life activities. Even in the modern science of medicine and in many of the newer statistical forms of analysis of human economics, this ancient cycle of human life is utilized as a fundamental scheme.

According to this primary cycle, human life is divided into a progression of periods, each period lasting approximately seven complete sun years or seven years of approximately 365 days each.

Merely as an illustration of how this simple cycle manifests itself, and not to use this cycle as a part of the system to be explained later on, I will call your attention to the fact that we can easily divide our lives into periods of seven years, and notice how each period has brought its definite results or produced effects upon our growth, development, and mastership.

PERIOD NO. 1
Birth to 7th Year

Consider the first period of seven years. This is the time during which our babyhood and early youth occurs, and when

— 39 —

the fundamentals of our education and cultural development are laid. It is really a period of self-discovery, as far as the objective material world and our relation to it are concerned. We learn to walk and talk, control our bodies, and relate ourselves properly to our physical and material environments.

PERIOD NO. 2
7th to 14th Year

In this period certain physical changes take place in our development, and the mental side of our nature takes a secondary place in the changes going on. It is just before the fulfillment of the second period that the important physical changes in both the male and female occur, preparing the child for the third stage. If these changes do not occur before the end of the second period, the child is psychologically and physiologically subnormal, and both physiology and psychology have unconsciously recognized this second period in the cycle of life.

PERIOD NO. 3
14th to 21st Year

In this period the physical changes drop back into secondary place together with the mental, and the psychic side of human nature is developed primarily. This brings about the sense of responsibility, giving dignity, poise, and character to the individual. It is during this process that the individual attains that degree of psychic or psychological, as well as mental and physiological development, that establishes the individual as a capable entity, qualified to assume legal responsibilities. The person who does not attain this degree by the 21st year is backward in the progress that should have been made, and is classified as subnormal.

PERIOD No. 4
21st to 28th Year

In this period there is a development strongly centered in the emotional nature carrying on the unfoldment of the emotional spark that was awakened in the preceding period. During these years, the individual acquires stability, a further sense of responsibility, a softening of the nature, and a gradual activity in those higher, dormant faculties known as intuition, mental telepathy, unconscious psychometry, and similar psychic faculties, together with an awakening interest in music, art, language, and what may be termed the religious and higher things in life. An absence of any manifestation of the development of these faculties during this period would indicate to the psychologist or psychiatrist a subnormal development.

PERIOD NO. 5
28th to 35th Year

In this period we find the creative processes of the mind most active, and the ability to visualize, imagine, and mentally create greatly developed, with a developing attunement with the Cosmic Consciousness and the ethical standards of life. It is during this period that the greatest inventors have made most progress, and the business man has become energetic and successful. It is also noteworthy that it is during this period that many of the world's greatest philosophers, avatars, and mystics found the sudden Cosmic Illumination which is called *complete attunement* with the

Cosmic Consciousness. The greatest of these have begun their world-wide missions and written their greatest works during this period.

PERIOD NO. 6
35th to 42nd Year

In this period people enter a stage of development that induces the desire to explore, investigate, and reveal great knowledge and the hidden facts of life. A restlessness comes into their nature which makes them dissatisfied with the monotony of selfish and personal attainment, and quickens in their being the humanitarian and brotherly emotion which makes them want to share what they have with the world. Yet even if they have little else than time and knowledge to share, they want to explore or discover and bring these revealed things to the masses for their benefit.

It is during this period that people start disposing of great wealth that they have accumulated or inherited by building libraries or contributing to the arts, the sciences, schools, colleges, universities, or explorative and inventive expeditions and speculations. It is truly the culminating period of all the years that have preceded in the life of the average human being, and starts the system of compensation in the average individual's life whereby the individual feels the need of returning to the Cosmic and to mankind some of the benefits he has enjoyed.

PERIOD NO. 7
42nd to 49th Year

In this period the desire to rest, meditate, and philosophically speculate builds up in the human being a new chapter, which unfolds strongly and uniquely in each case until the individual becomes a new person with new hopes, new desires, a new viewpoint in life, and a new goal and ideal toward which to labor. The mind is turned more strongly toward religion and philosophy than to business. It is also turned to those humanitarian activities that bring consolation and peace, by giving help, health, and happiness to the downtrodden, disconsolate, or despondent. So surely does this period work out in the average person's life, to some degree, that one may easily judge the approximate age of any eminent character by noting the tendencies of his habits and the trend of his thoughts, even when such a person is in very moderate circumstances and can do nothing more than wish he were able to do the things that he has in his mind and heart.

PERIOD NO. 8
49th to 56th Year

In this period we find a tendency toward further retirement from personal or selfish ambition, accompanied by a gradual lessening of the vitality and physical prowess, but compensated for by a highly attuned psychic and mental nature. Here the pendulum is beginning to swing from the building up of a physical being to the building up of a spiritual being, and for this reason the physical body begins to lose its power to combat disease and to surmount the strains of accidents and undue strains upon the vitality. Vital statistics prepared by insurance companies and government bureaus plainly show the great changes in the physical body which take place during this period and the preceding one as the pendulum begins to swing from the physical to the spiritual.

PERIOD NO. 9
56th to 63rd Year

In this period there is a continuation of the conditions in the preceding period, but accompanied now by a mellowing of the mental faculties together with the weakening of the physical prowess, leaving the individual more and more a psychic and spiritual being in harmony with the entire purpose of the cycle of progression. As man is born to become a living soul, and not merely a soul-animated physical body, so he evolves, period by period, from birth to his 63rd year, from a physical being to a spiritual being, thereby approaching more closely the inevitable purpose of his existence.

* * *

The other periods of seven years each contribute to the spiritual development and the gradual breaking down of the physical body. The end of the cycles is approximately at the 144th year, in order that the cycle of life may harmonize with other cycles and other periods which will be dealt with later.

Thus we can see in this very simple cycle of seven-year periods a rhythm of life that is universal for all and in accordance with a mathematical or geometrical plan that is incomprehensible unless we study all of the cosmic laws and know, as the Rosicrucians do in their higher teachings, the universal scheme of cosmic rhythm.

One question may be asked here: "If this is a universal cycle with all beings, will it manifest the same effects in the lives of those who live in less-developed sections of the world as it does with those who live in more modernized areas? In answer to this we can only say that observation has shown that the cycle manifests its effects in every human being in accordance with the individual's progress through the larger cycles of universal life. In other words, the manifestations in each individual's life are in accordance with his or her stage of evolutionary development. Whether one believes in the doctrine of reincarnation or not, one cannot deny the effects of hereditary evolution, or the evolutionary effects of progressive generations.

Each generation of human beings of a normal type is brought to a higher degree of susceptibility to the influence of these cycles of life. To people in less-developed areas, the various periods outlined above would bring only such manifestations and changes in their nature as would be in keeping with their stage of evolution—or, in other words, in keeping with their degree of progress along the higher cycles of universal life.

In a lesser degree, there is considerable variation in these manifestations among those who are of one nation and in even the most enlightened part of the world. For instance, here in America there are those who more definitely and more clearly manifest the effects of these periods of the cycle in their lives than others, and even a casual investigation of the lives of these persons will show that one is more highly evolved along the universal lines of cultural development than the other.

We may compare these seven-year periods of the cycle to the individual notes of the octave on the piano. Each octave has its notes, separated into definite periods or rates of vibrations, and the periods in one octave are identical with the periods in another octave. We may say, then, that a less-developed person living through a cycle of life that is comparable to one of the lower octaves on the piano key-board, and although he passes through the periodic notes of that cycle, they do not manifest through him the same attunement or tone with harmonic vibrations that another person would manifest who might be passing through one of the higher octaves.

According to the doctrine of reincarnation and according to the doctrine of the evolution of character and personality, each human being passes through successive cycles like progressing through the various octaves of the keyboard from the lowest to the highest. We have no consciousness of what is the lowest octave, and we can have no consciousness of what may be the highest octave, or the last, if any, of the cycles of life. Life itself is continuous and immortal, and therefore it can have neither any beginning nor any ending.

Again I must call your attention to the fact that to attempt to think even of the beginning or the ending of the cycles of life, or of these cycles as having an endurance in time, is to attempt to reduce our comprehension to a time consciousness, which is purely a relative thing of the finite and not of the infinite. This is explained in the preceding chapter of this book.

CHAPTER 6

THE YEARLY CYCLE OF HUMAN LIFE
With Description of Cycle No. 2

IN the foregoing chapter I outlined the life cycle of each human being covering approximately 144 years and divided into periods of seven years each. Now we have another cycle to deal with, which we will refer to in the system explained later in this book as Cycle No. 2. This cycle has to do with our personal worldly affairs each year.

Cycle No. 2 is 365 days in length, or in other words, renews itself and starts over again at each one of our birthday anniversaries. Therefore, the duration of Cycle No. 2 is from birthday to birthday. This cycle is divided into seven periods, each having approximately 52 days and a few hours, or in other words, 52 1/7 days. This means that each year of our lives, from birthday to birthday, is divided into seven periods during which certain conditions are favorable or unfavorable for the things we wish to do and must do in the course of our earthly existence.

This cycle is somewhat complex, and yet if my reader will follow me closely and refer to the tables and illustrations given in this chapter, he will have no trouble in understanding and utilizing Cycle No. 2 to aid him in attainment of self-mastership.

As stated above, Cycle No. 2 runs from birthday to birthday. It has nothing to do with the yearly calendar or the year of the calendar that begins in January and ends on the last day of December. This means that each individual has a cycle all his own. The only way in which two or more persons may have the same cycle would be through these persons having been born on the same day.

If you were born, for instance, on March 20, then your yearly cycle is from March 20 to the following March 19, each year of your life. With a person born on June 2, his cycle would run from June 2 to the following June 1. This point must be kept in mind so that there is no confusion with the calendar year that runs from January to January; we must also keep in mind that this cycle has nothing to do with the astrological periods that begin and end around the 21st to the 23rd of each month.

Therefore, in figuring the seven periods of each of your yearly cycles, you must begin by dividing your years into sections of approximately 52 days each. If you were born, for instance, on March 20, you would begin with that day and count forward 52 days and then another 52 and another 52, and so on. Do the same if you were born on June 2, or on any other day.

For your convenience in figuring these periods, I am introducing here in these pages a calendar of 365 days of the year. This calendar is sufficiently accurate in its number of days to use for any year, regardless of whether the year is a leap year or not. You will note that the days of the months run consecutively after the name of each month. This makes it a simple matter to figure out the 52-day periods of your personal life cycle, or Cycle No. 2.

CHART A
CALENDAR FOR ANY YEAR

	1	2	3	4	5	6	7	8	9	10	11	12	13	14	15	16	17	18	19	20	21	22	23	24	25	26	27	28	29	30	31
January	1	2	3	4	5	6	7	8	9	10	11	12	13	14	15	16	17	18	19	20	21	22	23	24	25	26	27	28	29	30	31
February	1	2	3	4	5	6	7	8	9	10	11	12	13	14	15	16	17	18	19	20	21	22	23	24	25	26	27	28	29*		
March	1	2	3	4	5	6	7	8	9	10	11	12	13	14	15	16	17	18	19	20	21	22	23	24	25	26	27	28	29	30	31
April	1	2	3	4	5	6	7	8	9	10	11	12	13	14	15	16	17	18	19	20	21	22	23	24	25	26	27	28	29	30	
May	1	2	3	4	5	6	7	8	9	10	11	12	13	14	15	16	17	18	19	20	21	22	23	24	25	26	27	28	29	30	31
June	1	2	3	4	5	6	7	8	9	10	11	12	13	14	15	16	17	18	19	20	21	22	23	24	25	26	27	28	29	30	
July	1	2	3	4	5	6	7	8	9	10	11	12	13	14	15	16	17	18	19	20	21	22	23	24	25	26	27	28	29	30	31
August	1	2	3	4	5	6	7	8	9	10	11	12	13	14	15	16	17	18	19	20	21	22	23	24	25	26	27	28	29	30	31
September	1	2	3	4	5	6	7	8	9	10	11	12	13	14	15	16	17	18	19	20	21	22	23	24	25	26	27	28	29	30	
October	1	2	3	4	5	6	7	8	9	10	11	12	13	14	15	16	17	18	19	20	21	22	23	24	25	26	27	28	29	30	31
November	1	2	3	4	5	6	7	8	9	10	11	12	13	14	15	16	17	18	19	20	21	22	23	24	25	26	27	28	29	30	
December	1	2	3	4	5	6	7	8	9	10	11	12	13	14	15	16	17	18	19	20	21	22	23	24	25	26	27	28	29	30	31

*In Leap Years there are 29 days in February.

CHART B
EXAMPLES OF CYCLE No. 2 OR No. 3
STARTING ON NOVEMBER 25

Period No. 1	Nov. 25 to Jan. 16	1st Period, Nov. 25 to Jan. 16
Period No. 2	Jan. 17 to Mar. 8	2nd Period, Jan. 17 to Mar. 8
Period No. 3	Mar. 9 to Apr. 30	3rd Period, Mar. 9 to Apr. 30
Period No. 4	May 1 to June 21	4th Period, May 1 to June 21
Period No. 5	June 22 to Aug. 12	5th Period, June 22 to Aug. 12
Period No. 6	Aug. 13 to Oct. 3	6th Period, Aug. 13 to Oct. 3
Period No. 7	Oct. 4 to Nov. 24	7th Period, Oct. 4 to Nov. 24

(NOTE: Either one of the above methods of tabulating the periods of a cycle may be used, in accordance with the instructions given on these pages.)

Let us take an illustration now of a person born on November 25. His yearly cycle begins on the November 25 and ends on November 24 of each year. We will start, therefore, with the calendar and write on a piece of paper the date, November 25, and begin to figure the first period of 52 days by counting on the lines of the calendar 52 days forward from November 25.

First we count five days to the end of November and then begin with December 1 as the sixth day. Continuing through to the end of December gives us 36 days, so we continue counting in January and find that the 52nd day falls on January 16. Therefore, we write on our piece of paper opposite November 25 the date January 16, and then opposite this, "First Period." This means that for a person born on November 25, the first period of his yearly cycle is from November 25 to January 16.

To find the second period of 52 days we start again at January 16 and count forward through January and February and partly into March until we have counted off 52 more days, which we find brings us to March 8. So we write on the paper again under the first line, the two dates, January 17 to March 8, and right opposite this, "Second Period."

Again we begin with March 8 and count forward 52 days, which brings us to April 30. We write down the dates again, March 9 to April 30, and put opposite it, "Third Period." Continuing this way we find that the fourth period is from May 1 to June 21. And the fifth period is from June 22 to August 12. The sixth period is from August 13 to October 3, and the seventh period October 4 to November 24.

These dates are approximate because we are laying aside the few hours that should be added each day to make the exact period of 52 1/7 days—or 52 days, 3 hours, and 24 minutes. If any of the periods are minus one day or plus one day, it will not make any serious difference in the application of the system. If your last period of 52 days falls a day ahead of your birthday, this will make no difference in the use of the system.

With a person born on February 8, the first period would be from the February 8 to April 1, by counting 52 days from February 8. And the second period would end on the May 23 by counting 52 days from April 1. To figure out these periods in your life is not a difficult matter, and it is not a mathematical matter so long as you have the calendar to use conveniently. The important thing to bear in mind is to write on a piece of paper the seven periods of your year, and to number these periods from one to seven. These you should call your second cycle periods.

I am going to give you a third cycle shortly that is also very important, and it is divided into seven periods also. Those periods will be called the third cycle periods, and they must not be confused with the second cycle periods or the first cycle periods outlined in Chapter 5.

Now each of these periods in Cycle No. 2 contains opportunities, conditions, urges, influences, temptations, and cosmic effects which have an important and subtle bearing upon the success or failure, strength or weakness, joy or sorrow, of your personal affairs. I will now outline these things below.

PERIOD NO. 1

This is a period when a person should utilize every personal power and ability to advance his own interests among persons of influence who have powers or privileges to grant or give. It is a period when solicitation should be made for favors, either in seeking employment, benefits, loans, partnerships, investments, special concessions, releases, or even favors in the form of time or postponements or dismissals in court. It is an especially good period to seek favors or honors, help or recognition, from persons who are in high power or high positions such as government officials, judges, mayors, governors, senators, people at the head of large corporations or big business, or persons who hold valuable papers, documents, and matters that may be of great importance, and which may be released, modified, or otherwise affected by your solicitation.

This is also a good period for advancing one's own personal self among the populace, or with the people of your city, state, or country, or in building up your credit standing or your reputation with newspapers and influential people. It is a time to push yourself forward with discrimination and yet determination, for all of the cosmic vibrations are in favor of boosting and helping you personally so far as your name, reputation, honor, and integrity among high persons or the multitudes are concerned.

PERIOD NO. 2

This period is distinctly different from the foregoing period, for during these 52 days everything will tend to be favorably directed toward your plans regarding any journeys, especially those that are not for many months' or a year's duration, but those that are short, quick, and of immediate importance rather than of importance in the future. Journeys by water or by train are generally favored during this period. It is also an excellent time for moving your home to a new location, or moving your business, or moving your occupation, if it is something under your own control. In other words, this is a period for changes which are quick and soon over with.

In a business way this period will be found very favorable for such activities pertaining to movable things, and things of indefinite location. The moving of freight or the dealing with freight business, expressage, automobiles, wagons, carriages, trucks, public conveyances, public lectures, shows, performances, and things of this kind will be found successful. Strange to say, this period is also an excellent one for those who are dealing with liquids, chemicals, milk, water, water power, gasoline, or other things of a liquid nature. Dealing with people who are in lines of business associated with all of the foregoing will also be more successful in this period than in any other.

Inversely, one should not plan a change of business or start a new career in business or attempt to build a permanent thing upon any change that is made during this period. Moving one's home may be successful if done during this period, but at the same time the buying of a new home during this period will be very apt to result in a future change because a change made during this particular period does not make for permanency. Therefore, all things done during this time should be of such a nature as to begin during the period and end shortly afterward or as to be of the present months or year rather than the future.

This period is also good for persons who are in business such as catering to transients, or to fluctuating business affairs, such as those who conduct hotels, or traffic, or who cater to persons who are constantly moving or passing by. It is also a good period in which to engage new employees or servants, or to begin any agricultural developments or planting. Contracts, agreements, legal papers, and other business affairs that are intended to continue over a period of years or remain permanent matters should not be started or completed during this period.

It is an unfavorable period in which to loan money or even borrow money, and is not good for the construction of any building or the starting of any business that has a considerable investment to last over a long period. Certainly it is an unfavorable period to speculate in the stock market or to gamble in any form.

PERIOD NO. 3

Here we have a period that may be fortunate or unfortunate according to the application of the cosmic powers, and the discretion and discrimination that a person uses. This period fills the individual with an almost uncontrollable impulse to want to do great and important things, and the fiery energy that goes through the human system during this period wants to express itself in many ways. If directed carefully, this period can be one of the greatest in the whole year for the building up of a business and the accomplishment of those things that call for great physical energy, physical effort, endurance, vitality, determination, and persistency.

On the other hand, if the energy is misspent, or applied without discrimination and judgment, great tasks may be undertaken or started that will not be completed in a long time, and too much for one person may be started through the restless energy that wants to express itself. This is an excellent period in which to overcome those obstacles and conditions that in the past periods seemed to check every advancement because of the energy and labor required.

It is an excellent period to begin anything that has to start with a bang and have a great impulse during the first month or two of its career. Certainly this is an excellent period for dealing with affairs of the army, the navy, military engineering, munitions, or with those persons or lines of business that deal with heavy muscular or extreme vital energy. It is likewise an excellent period for the building up of a business or interests dealing with iron, steel, cutlery, sharp instruments, or things connected with electrical machinery, furnaces, and fire.

It is also a fine period in which to deal with enemies, competitors, and rivals, who have heretofore been obstacles in the path, but it is a poor time to attempt to master those obstacles or persons with arguments or with contracts, papers, or agreements. If sheer energy, persistency, and long hours of activity and hard work will affect competitors or obstacles in the way, this is the period in which to overcome them in this manner.

It is during this period that many quarrels, arguments, and business strifes occur, and these should be avoided because they are not apt to end very successfully for any person involved. It is an excellent period for salesmen or lecturers or others who must depend upon very forceful oratory or fiery argument to convince.

PERIOD NO. 4

This period is considerably different from the preceding one, inasmuch as in it we have the cosmic forces strongly influencing and strengthening the mental, nervous, and psychic side of the nature rather than the physical. It is an excellent period for the writing and mental creation of books, plays, plans, business schemes, and other matters requiring a fertile mind, quick thinking, smooth-flowing language, and an unusual ability to express the thoughts in the mind. In fact, the mind will seem to be highly charged with new thoughts, new ideas, and easily contacted expressions of the Cosmic Mind.

Incidentally, it has been noticed that since the mind is very fertile and very sensitive during this period, ideas, impulses, and urges are apt to flow into the mental consciousness very rapidly. To take advantage of most of these, the person must act upon impulse and quickly grasp the ideas and put them into practical application before others crowd them out. Therefore, it is is a dependable period for acting upon impulses or so-called intuitive hunches. The nature of the person becomes optimistic and, because of the mental activity, somewhat nervous and restless, with the imagination highly charged.

It is a good period in which to deal with literary persons, reporters, messengers, to engage stenographers and writers, bookkeepers, engravers, artists, and persons whose work is primarily mental and rapid in expression. Artists are more inspired and more nimble in their work during this time.

A warning must be given here, however, that great deceptions can be practiced upon persons during this period. Stories, reports, papers, documents, or other written or spoken matter that may come to your attention during this period must be carefully analyzed before being accepted, because it is a period when falsehood is as nimble and eloquently expressed in words or writing as is the truth. Deception, therefore, is not only very easy, but very frequent. Forgeries in regard to personal and business papers, and counterfeits of important papers or money must be watched at this time. Many of the great losses in life through thievery, robbery, or deception occur during this period, and proper precaution should be taken to prevent these things.

It is a good time for study and for the absorption of special knowledge and for the building up of a quick and nimble mind and tongue. It is not a good time to enter into marriage, to hire servants, or to return from a long journey or to buy homes, business propositions, or lands.

PERIOD NO. 5

Here we enter into what may be called the success period of each year, as far as our personal, private affairs are concerned. During these 52 days the cosmic impulses and tendencies are to bring happy fruition and successful termination of the things with which we have been laboring, or the things we have planned or put into action. It is during this time that our personal affairs expand, grow, and increase in prosperity. The mind of the person becomes filled with higher ideas of courtesy, religion, science, and law, and there is a tendency toward good fellowship, sociability, benevolence, honesty, and sympathy.

It is an excellent period for dealing with lawyers or judges of the court, government officials, clergymen, physicians, merchants, or people of wealth. It is also a good period in which to begin a long journey in contradistinction to the good period for short journeys which occurs during the second period of this cycle. This is also a very fine period for renewing or starting interests in philosophical works, metaphysical studies, the preparation of sermons, or legal briefs, or those things requiring very favorable influences to bring to a successful issue.

For that reason it is a fine time in which to collect money that is owing or to buy for the purpose of selling, and to sell or speculate or even to borrow. Any attempts during this period, however, to deal with tricky affairs that are not legitimate speculations, or to deal with cattle, to buy or sell cattle, or to deal with meat products on a large scale, or to deal with marine affairs, will prove unsuccessful.

PERIOD NO. 6

Here is a period that may be called the holiday of the year. It is a time for pleasure, amusement, relaxation, and entertainment. This does not mean, however, that business will not prosper and that regular affairs of life should be withheld or modified during this period, for all things that are legitimate and good will continue with almost as much success as during the preceding period. However, this is the time in which to deal specifically with certain affairs of life with more intensity than at other periods.

Now is the time to make long or short visits for relaxation or for the renewing of friendships. It is a fine period for dealing with women, or for women to deal with men in the pleasurable things of life, and in the higher things of life. It is especially fortunate for such business matters as deal with the higher and more pleasant things of life such as with art, music, poetry, painting, sculpting, personal adornments, perfumes, incense, flowers, and so forth. Short journeys will be happy and successful during this time but not long voyages, or in fact any voyages by water.

This is a good period for the consummation of transactions of a speculative nature, or to buy stocks and bonds or to engage employees and assistants.

PERIOD NO. 7

This is the critical and disruptive period of life each year. I feel sure that after you have outlined the yearly cycle of your life for each year, if you will then look back over the last ten or more years of your life and note the things that occurred during the seventh period of each of your years, that you will see how true this is. It is that sort of a period when devolution precedes evolution, or when the breaking down begins in order that there may be a new building up. It is like the period when the house is torn down, brick by brick, and leveled in order to rebuild again.

In one sense it is disruptive, and in another sense it is the first stage to reconstruction. For that reason, each should be warned to take advantage of the natural tendency of this period and at the same time guard against these tendencies that they may not go too far, or that one may not wrongly labor and run counter with the tendencies instead of cooperating with them. It is the period when most things that have been hanging fire and are about to end, or disrupt, do so. If a business or any other affair has been going poorly and has shown a tendency to fail, and go to pieces, this is the period when such a culmination is most apt to occur. If this result is not wanted, care must be exercised not to do those things which will help to bring it about The mind is very apt to become despondent, discouraged, or pessimistic during this period, and that must be kept in mind, for if this attitude is allowed to affect the actions in business or in personal affairs, it will help to bring about a disastrous result.

The influences during this period are very subtle, and must be carefully analyzed and reasoned before being applied. We have said that during the fourth period of this cycle the rapidity with which ideas come to the mind, along with the cosmic influences creating them, makes it advisable to be quick and even impulsive in accepting and applying these ideas. The very reverse is true in the present period. Impulsiveness here will bring disaster. If matters that are pending or ideas that suggest themselves can be postponed and held over until past the coming birthday, and put into the first period or the second period of this cycle, it will assure greater success.

This is a good period for dealing with elderly persons, judges, referees, or persons who must debate and consider carefully and for a long time before rendering their decisions. It is also a good time for business interests dealing with inventions and mechanical things, and even for applying for patents or government papers of protection. It is a very good period for dealing in real estate, mines, and minerals, and those things that are of the earth, and deeply seated in it, or in hidden or out-of-the-way places. For that reason it is a good period to deal with persons engaged in lines of business connected with these things, or with grain or fruits of the earth.

Certainly it is the most unfavorable period in the whole year for starting anything new or launching a new business or giving a new impulse or new expenditure in business except for protective purposes. Voyages by sea, long or short, or on land, should be avoided unless their effects are to result in weeks and months of the future when they will fall in another period.

* * *

Thus we have the seven periods of Cycle No. 2. The influences operating during each one of these periods may not begin on the first day of each period, nor end the last day of each period. In fact, the influences of each period may begin a few days before the period, and lap over a few days into the succeeding period. For this reason the precise hour or part of the day in which each period begins is not important. The only way to be sure that you have the best influences of each period is to avoid the first and last two days of each period in doing anything of a very definite nature pertaining to that period, because at the beginning and ending of each of these periods there is a mixed influence of the preceding and succeeding one.

CHAPTER 7

PERIODS OF THE BUSINESS CYCLE
With Description of Cycle No. 3

E ARLIER in this book I stated that everything that has a beginning in the worldly plan of existence starts its career in accordance with a cycle of progression just as the human life begins a cycle at birth. Just how long such cycles may last or continue to manifest depends upon many things, and just as human life on this plane may last for a month, a year, 30 years, or 80 or more, so a business proposition or an institution or a commercial plan may have a life of activity covering a month or a year or a score of years. However long it may operate or continue to exist, its existence will be in accordance with a cycle of progression that is just as definite as the cycle of progression of human life.

In other words, if several people unite today to organize and incorporate a new business under a new name, to carry on a new line of activity, and the new name of the company and its new plans are adopted and definitely completed today, then this new business would have its birthday today, and would begin its career today, and would have a cycle of progression beginning with today, just as though these persons had given birth to a human form with a soul.

Each one of our business institutions, business schemes, plans, or forms of activity, has a birthday. In other words, there is some day in the year that is passing that constitutes the day on which the business first started, or first made its representations to the public, or began its material activities.

Most businesses operating today can easily determine what day of the month in the years that are past they began their activities, but the so-called fiscal year should have nothing to do with the determination of the birthday of a business. Many businesses that actually began their career in June, July, or August have made their fiscal year run from September to September, or from January to January. If the beginning of the fiscal year is used as the true birthdate of the company, a mistake may be made in working out the periods of each year. It is not absolutely necessary to have the precise or exact date of the starting of the business or proposition, whatever it may be, as long as one can select the day of the beginning approximately. In other words, a variation of two or three days will not make any difference.

Important points to bear in mind in determining what is the true birthday of a business are as follows: The day on which the company received its incorporation charter is not as important as the day on which the company began its business affairs in dealing with the public. The day on which a number of persons gathered together and decided to start a business and actually selected the name and officers of the business is a more correct birthday than the day on which the first announcement was made to the public or the first article was sold. In smaller lines of business, the day on which a store or factory was rented and the work of installing equipment or furnishings was started would be the birthday of the business. The day on which a person gave up his other affairs and began to plan and work out a new proposition would be a more correct birthday than the day on which he actually sold or handled any of the products of his business.

If a business has had a formal opening with a formal announcement of the opening, and a reception of the public, and a definite start of the business in a formal way, then this day would be the birthday of a business. With a business that has changed hands or changed its name, the date on which the firm began to operate with the new name or with the new owners would be the birthdate of the present business, regardless of how long it had been operating under the older name. Thus we see that some little thought must be given to the determination of what is the approximate birthday of a business.

When we speak of business, we mean not only stores which sell merchandise of any nature whatsoever at retail, but also of factories and manufacturing businesses, brokerage firms, real estate offices, professional businesses such as those of physicians, artists, musicians, and others in similar lines. A birthday may be the opening of the office of a lawyer or adviser of any kind, or the opening of a mail order or sales proposition, the starting of a canvassing or selling plan, or any scheme or definite operation that has to do with commercial or business activities, wherein either a group of persons or only one person is involved.

Having determined, therefore, the approximate birthday of any business or proposition of a material business nature, one should proceed as with the marking of the periods of the cycle of human life. In other words, start with the approximate date of birth and write down on a piece of paper the periods of 52 days each. Let us say a person or group of people started the manufacturing of a piece of machinery. Let us say that the business was born on the day when the partners came together and deposited their money in a bank and decided to go into business together and selected a name for their firm. Let us say that this date was approximately June 3, 1914. June 3 of each year would be the anniversary of the birthday of the concern.

Starting, therefore, with June 3, we would count off on the calendar given on the preceding pages 52 days from June 3. This would give us July 25 as the date of the end of the first period, and the beginning of the second period. Counting off another 52 days, we would write the end of the second period on the piece of paper and so on until we had written down the dates of the beginning and ending of the seven periods in each yearly cycle of the business.

Now in each of these seven periods various cosmic influences, urges, tendencies, and impulses would affect the affairs of the business, just as though that business were a human entity. Since the business itself depends upon the actions and reactions of human nature on the part of the public, and those officers and persons directing the business, so we find the business itself is reacting to the impulses, urges, and tendencies of the complexity of the human nature involved. This enables us, therefore, to analyze the trend of each business proposition, and to discover that it has certain favorable and unfavorable periods during which the best interests of the business may be protected, advanced, modified, or conserved.

Let me present, therefore, a brief analysis of what each business of any nature whatsoever may expect during the seven periods of its yearly cycle.

PERIOD NO. 1

During the first 52 days of the yearly cycle of each business, beginning with its birthday and covering the 52 days following, each business will find greater success in all forms of promotion that solicit or depend for their success upon the good will and the preferment of the public. It is not as excellent a period for the actual building up of sales and return of money as it is a period for securing approval, favor, recognition, and general good will.

This would be the period to solicit endorsements or high recognition by eminent persons and concerns that would either result eventually in sales through such persons, or in giving widespread publicity and advertising to the concern. It is also an excellent period in which to advertise a business widely, not so much for direct sales as to build up prestige and public recognition.

It is a good period for the sending forth of emissaries, representatives, or high members of the firm to meet other eminent persons in the business world and, therefore, secure recognition and high favor. For this reason it is an excellent period to deal with government officials, judges of the court, or senators, or congressmen from whom you desire preferment, special favors, or the passage of protective bills or regulations. This makes the period also good for the securing of political influence, political cooperation, and recognition. The thought of the concern during this period should be not of money, but of name, reputation, and prestige.

PERIOD NO. 2

During this period any firm or business of any nature will find that it is a good time to make important changes of a temporary nature in regard to important employees, modifications in business practice, temporary locations, and for trying out short-time plans and propositions. On the other hand, it is a very unfavorable period during which to make any new agreements, any new plans of a definite nature, or to enter into any contracts or agreements of any kind unless they are reduced to writing, and properly sealed and signed so as to give them a long-time standing. Verbal agreements and arrangements entered into at this time are apt to be cast aside quickly and changed very rapidly or suddenly, and amount to nothing. It is also a good period for the building up of business friendships, and every business firm would do well to take advantage of this period to contact new and prospective customers in a friendly way, for business friendships of a very helpful nature have generally been built up during this period.

PERIOD NO. 3

Here we have a period of construction and great energizing power. It is during this period that any business proposition should be pushed to its utmost. Every facility and every means of manufacturing, selling, producing, advertising, promoting, and extending the business should be adopted and utilized to the utmost during this period. It is also a good period for the arrangement of plans for collections, or to send out collectors or letters intended to collect money, but it is not a good period for attempting to fight any issues in court that have to do with the activities of business enemies, business rivals, or business competition. Other legal matters, however, may be pushed at this period, and will generally receive more favorable reaction than at any other period, especially if the matter is one that calls for the expenditure of a great deal of energy and of considerable fighting for the protection of certain issues or rights.

On the other hand, every firm and business should watch out for dangerous accidents, disasters, and troubles through enemies, through fires, or through sudden explosions of wrath, enmity, or hatred during this period. Manufacturing plants and other propositions should be careful of fires or explosions from fires, gases, and stored-up energies of any kind during this period. It is during this period also that personal enemies of the business will attempt to wreck it or even to injure the character or life of a person connected with a business, if the business has attained any degree of enmity on the part of competitors or others.

It is a very good period for dealing with army and navy matters, the military departments of the government, engineering, munitions, machinery, or firms or individuals associated with these.

PERIOD NO. 4

This is the period in which any firm or business would do well to enter into its largest campaign of widespread advertising, whether this be nationwide advertising or the mere solicitation by letter of customers in a limited area. Whatever writing, planning, and scheming of promotion a business firm or individual may want to do in any year of its business, it will be found to be most successful during this period of the business cycle of each year. On the other hand, it is also an excellent period for the drawing up of new contracts, new agreements, papers of incorporation, documents, transfers, and so forth.

It is an excellent period to deal with newspapermen, diplomats, arbitrators, or others who can use their mentalities or printed or written words to further the interests of the concern. On the other hand, firms must be careful during this period to watch out for deception by word of mouth or writing, for forgeries, and for tricky agreements or plans cleverly presented and which are apt to have a serious reaction in many ways.

PERIOD NO. 5

Here is a period of growth and financial success for any concern or business proposition. This is the period in which to seek investment, or seek to secure credit and extend the time in which payments must be made or negotiations closed. It is one of the best periods in the business year for selling, and the actual distribution of material on a sales basis, if immediate results and a quick and fair return of money are desired. It is an excellent period in which to collect bad or old debts, and it is an excellent time in which to bring matters into court where the favorable decision desired hangs by a slender thread. For all things being quick and right, this period is favorable to a constructive and just decision.

It is an excellent period also for the promotion of the business into foreign lands or distant places or with large concerns that deal in international matters or have international distribution and sales agreements. It seems to be an especially good period for business firms to promote their affairs with railroad, railway, and electric companies, and with all companies and concerns that deal in things that cater to the pleasures and happiness of the public.

PERIOD NO. 6

This is the period in each year when every business should relax its activities if it finds it necessary to relax at all, and should plan its periods for the vacation or absence of any of its important directors or operators. It is also an excellent period for the promotion of certain branches of business such as those that deal with the art world, or with music, poetry, sculpting, artists' materials, women's clothing, or articles of adornment, beauty preparations, high-grade shoes, hosiery, evening wraps, hats, luxurious automobiles, oriental rugs, antique furniture, fine books, expensive musical instruments, concerts, operas, and other things representing the luxuries, refinements, and clean and wholesome pleasures of life. Therefore, it is well to push the sale of things of this nature during this period, or to promote good will or interest among persons who are associated with such lines of business.

This is an excellent period for the heads of a concern or the individual owner of any kind of business to make the acquaintance of his customers, and to make such intimate contacts with persons as may be helpful to the business or the individuals of the business in the near future. It is also a good period for the collection of money, the buying of stocks and bonds, or the promotion of the finances of the company through investment in conservative stocks of other concerns. Therefore, it would be an excellent period for the bringing about of partnerships, monopolistic corporations, and the formation of subsidiary associations and alliances of a similar nature.

PERIOD NO. 7

Here we have the reconstruction period for all business propositions, and during these last 52 days before the birthday of the concern or business, great care must be taken not to start any new line of activity or to go too heavily into advertising that is intended to build up a new department or a new phase of the business, or to do otherwise than cooperate with the cosmic tendencies to reconstruct. Since it is the period during which changes of a tearing down nature must be expected, it is a wrong period in which to plan to do reconstruction without the preliminary stage of tearing down. In other words, during this period no expansion must be expected unless it is associated in some way with a breaking down or tearing down process as a part of the reconstruction.

Since some form of breaking down and change is very apt to take place during these 52 days, every business concern or individual should see that any contemplated changes or tearing down processes that have been in mind are brought to issue during this time, and therefore permitted to expend themselves or manifest themselves while such a period is favorable. Certainly no new alliances, affiliations, partnerships, or agreements, contracts, or offers of agreement or contract should be made during this period.

It is an excellent time to consult with persons in retirement, or who have been in business and have retired, or with judges, referees, or advisers of any kind. All acts must be guarded with a conservative attitude, and extreme caution and providence manifested in every line of activity. Great diplomacy must be shown in every act, and every business should take advantage of this period to conserve its activities, hold steady to its line of progress, and not allow anything of a radical nature in either advertising, selling, buying, or planning to occur.

* * *

Thus we have an outline of the favorable and unfavorable influences, urges, and tendencies from the Cosmic during the seven periods of the yearly cycle of each business or form of business activity. You may test the occurrences of this outline by going back over your business affairs for several years, and noting in what periods of each year you had trouble with your competitors or with enemies, or in what periods of each year you have had the greatest sales and the most success in promotion, or the most disruptive and tearing down conditions to contend with.

You will soon find, if you review your business activities over a period of ten or more years, that your business affairs have naturally divided themselves into periods that agree with the outline given above. You will also notice, if you are keenly analytical, that in certain periods of the past when you have attempted to do certain things with your business, your plans have failed or the scheme you had in mind or started did not materialize as you expected, and you will see that it was because you started these things or planned these things in a period that was not favorable.

SELF-MASTERY AND FATE

CHAPTER 8

HOW TO USE THE PERIODS OF THE CYCLES

IN the foregoing chapters, two distinct cycles have been outlined. Cycle No. 2, explained in Chapter 6, relates to your own personal existence, and explains what tendencies and conditions will be fortunate or unfortunate for you during each of the seven periods that come between your birthdays. Cycle No. 3, presented in Chapter 7, pertains to the career of your business or any venture or proposition which you have created or which has been brought into birth at some definite time.

Now if you are a business man or woman, or employed in business, or venturing into some business, or have some proposition which you wish to carry on to success, you will find that you have two cycles to deal with: first, the cycle of your own personal life; and second, the cycle of the business or proposition in which you are interested. Each of these two cycles has seven periods to the year, and it is not often that the periods of each of these two cycles are coincidental. If your business or your business proposition was created and started on one of your birthdays, then its periods each year would run coincidentally with the periods of your own personal life. Otherwise, two periods of different conditions will confront you.

For instance, let us assume that you who are reading this book were born around June 1. And let us say that the business you are interested in is something that had its beginning around the preceding July 1. In trying to find out what you should do and should not do in your business and personal affairs during the next 30 or 60 days, you would find, if you tabulated the cycle of your business and the cycle of your personal life, that personally you are now in the first period of your yearly cycle, whereas your business would be in the seventh period of your business cycle.

In other words, your own personal tendencies, interests, and affairs would be affected by the conditions outlined in Period No. 1 of Cycle No. 2, in Chapter 6 of this book, and your business affairs would be influenced by the conditions explained in Period No. 7 of Cycle No. 3 outlined in Chapter 7 of this book. In trying to determine, therefore, what you should do at the present time, you would have to analyze and carefully study the conditions in Period No. 7 of Cycle No. 3, and the conditions in Period No. 1 of Cycle No. 2 pertaining to your personal life.

Whenever it occurs that the time in which you are interested, and about which you are consulting this system, brings your personal life and your business life into the same period, then you can easily understand what to do and what not to do. But, whenever the two periods are different, and you find opposing influences in each of the periods, you must blend them, analyze them, and decide for yourself what to do. It has been found that certain points will be helpful in this regard. If the business you are in is exclusively your own, then you may be guided by the conditions of your own personal life cycle, as more important and more dominating than the conditions in your business cycle, but the conditions of the business cycle should always be carefully watched by you, and the things that are unfavorable therein carefully avoided, regardless of what may be stated in the periods of your personal cycle.

If the business you are in, or the business matter in which you are interested, is not exclusively your own, but is a partnership, corporation, or a combination of interests of a number of individuals, then you must bear in mind that to make the business the most successful, you must follow its individual cycle and periods, regardless of your own periods or the periods of the other persons connected with the business.

There are many times in the affairs of big business men, and all successful business men and women of any degree, when personal desires, ambitions, success and profits must be laid aside in order that the business which they control may prosper and succeed. In other words, all persons who have had any real success in business at all will tell you that very often there have been opportunities, temptations, and inclinations in their lives for journeys abroad or long vacations, or other things that would profit them personally, help their health, and increase their knowledge and wisdom.

And yet with all of these things coming at opportune times, and with every temptation to yield to them, they have had to pass them by and sacrifice their own personal interests and opportunities solely because business affairs had a different trend and a different set of conditions. On the other hand, it is known that very often when conditions in business are most unfavorable or seemingly so, there are certain conditions in the personal life of an individual connected with that business that permit him to lay business aside and indulge in his own personal affairs with success and without serious injury to his business interests.

The important point to be considered always is whether your individual success, financial progress, and best interests in life are so related to your business affairs that both of them will suffer together, or both of them prosper together, or whether they can be so separated that you individually may prosper while the business may decline, and vice versa. Another important matter that must be considered is that in most cases your own personal cycle is of more importance to you and your connection with the business than the cycle of the business itself.

If you are merely an employee in business, then the cycle of the business with which you are connected is of little importance to you except insofar as you can work with it and help the business by taking advantage of its good periods. If, on the other hand, the only business you have is something that is owned and controlled by you and is your sole income, and you and your family are exclusively dependent upon it, then the business cycle becomes an important matter for your consideration.

If it occurs that in one period of your personal life cycle the conditions are such that it is indicated you should exert every possible energy to build and create more business, and push your business interests to the utmost, while at the same time the period of the business cycle indicates that you should let your business remain quiet and not push it too strongly, then the only thing for you to do is to use the conditions of your personal cycle to think, plan, and create new and better things for your business, but do not put them into effect until there is a good period in your business cycle when such things should be done.

The use of the system outlined in this book requires the careful admixture of the indications given in both the personal and business cycles. It calls for a careful study and analysis of the periods in each of these two cycles and a proper blending of them until you come to a conclusion as to what you should do and which of the influences and conditions are the most important. Again I would remind you of the fact that in the average case an individual's personal cycle is of more importance than the business cycle, but for corporations or big business combines where there are a number of people owning and directing the business, and where the business is an impersonal one, the business cycle should be given more consideration than the personal cycle of any one of the persons connected with the business.

In all the affairs of the home, of social interests, personal finances, personal plans and progress, the personal cycle is unquestionably the one to be followed above all others.

CHAPTER 9

THE PERIODS OF THE HEALTH CYCLE
With Description of Cycle No. 4

———————

FOR those who want to give special attention to their health during critical periods, or generally throughout the year, the following matter and that in Chapter 10 will be of considerable help.

The health cycle should be mapped out as are the preceding cycles, by starting with the birthday and dividing each year into seven periods of 52 days each.

The conditions in regard to health in each one of these periods of each year are as follows:

PERIOD NO. 1

During this period the vitality and constitutional health should be at its best and, if it is below normal, it will be more quickly and easily increased and strengthened by normal living and the avoidance of the violation of any natural laws. Plenty of outdoor walking, good air, drinking plenty of water and eating proper foods, avoiding foods that are overheating, especially the starches and raw or rare meats—this will yield results. The eyes should be guarded against overuse or use in bright electric lights or sunlight, and if any operation is planned, or system of health building is to be adopted, this is the period in which to start these things.

PERIOD NO. 2

This is a period in which many light and temporary physical conditions may affect the body, and passing emotional conditions affect the mind. In other words, during this period a person may have temporary trouble with the stomach, bowels, bloodstream, and nerves. These conditions seem to come quickly, last but a few days, and pass away quickly. None of these should be neglected; each should be given immediate attention, but there need be no anxiety regarding the continuance of such conditions if immediate attention is given, for all of the influences tend to bring rapid changes in the health and physical condition of the body during these 52 days. During this period there are apt to be days with headaches, upset stomachs, trouble with the eyes or the ears, catarrh, coughs, aches and pains through mild forms of cold, and with women occasionally aches and pains in the breasts and abdomen. During this period everyone should try to be cheerful and not permit the mind to dwell upon the temporary conditions that affect the body, but simply attend promptly to the checking of any condition that may arise and then cast it out of the mind.

PERIOD NO. 3

This is a period when accidents may happen, and often sudden operations come into one's life, of either a minor or major nature. Likewise, suffering by fire or injury through sharp instruments, falls, or sudden blows, is more likely during this period than any other. Persons should be careful of their food and not overeat, and the body should be kept normally warm because during this period there will be a tendency toward colds, often resulting from overeating or overheating the body. The bloodstream should be kept clean and the bowels active, so that blood conditions will not result in sores, boils, eczema, rashes, or other more serious conditions of the skin and blood. The blood pressure also should be watched during this period, for there will be a tendency for it to rise, and overwork or strain should be avoided. Any abnormal strain upon any part of the body is very apt to bring a breaking down during this period.

PERIOD NO. 4

During this period the nervous system of your body will be tried to its utmost and there will be many tendencies toward nervousness expressing itself in the functioning of various organs or in an outer form of restlessness and uneasiness. Too much study, reading, planning, or use of the mind and nervous system will surely bring definite reactions during this period. More sleep and more rest are required during this period than in any other part of the year. Fretfulness and nervousness may also affect the digestion, the functioning of the stomach, and may also produce a nervous heart which may cause misgivings and inconvenience. Persons who have been laboring too long or too tediously with mental problems or work requiring mental strain should be forced to relax and rest during this period, or a mental breakdown is inevitable.

PERIOD NO. 5

This is another good period, when the health should be very good, especially if normal living is indulged in, and the great outdoors utilized for deep breathing, fairly long walks, and good exercise. There will probably be a tendency during this period to overindulge in the things that please the flesh, such as the eating of preferred foods, elaborate meals and banquets, rich concoctions, spicy drinks, and so forth, and even overindulgence morally and ethically in many ways. All of this must be avoided during this period in order to prevent serious conditions. This is a good period in which to recover from fevers, chronic conditions, or other abnormal or subnormal conditions of the body which have been existing for some time. During this period, mental suggestions, metaphysical principles, and right thinking will have more effect upon the body and the health than at any other period.

PERIOD NO. 6

This period is another one in which overindulgence should be carefully avoided in regard to work, mental strain, eating, or any of the pleasures of the flesh. It is a period during which the skin, throat, internal generative system, and kidneys may become affected. Therefore, plenty of water should be drunk during this period, the bowels kept open, and rest with outdoor exercise should be indulged in more frequently than mental strain or overwork.

PERIOD NO. 7

This is the period during which chronic or lingering conditions are often contracted, and which remain a long time and cause considerable trouble in overcoming. Everyone should be especially careful of catching colds or contracting serious contagious fevers during this period by avoiding the places where such things may be contacted. The mind and whole nature is very apt to be despondent and below normal in the ability to ward off and fight an incoming condition.

Even the bloodstream may be lowered in its vitality at this period and, therefore, is unable to fight even the normal amount of germs or unfavorable influences that generally come in contact with every human being.

It is not a good time, however, for taking medicine or having an operation performed, or for starting any new or drastic method of improving the health unless in an emergency or unless it is to be continued over a long period, so that its real effect will come into the next period of 52 days, which will be Period No. 1 of the next cycle. The eyes, the ears, and in fact any one of the five senses may become affected during this period, and care should be taken that colds or other conditions do not linger during this period or continue without proper expert attention. It is one of the most serious periods of the whole year for each person, in regard to diseases and chronic conditions.

CHAPTER 10

THE CYCLES OF DISEASE AND SEX

A S stated in a previous paragraph, the laws and principles set forth in this book have naught to do with the art and practice of the system called *astrology*, and whether one believes that the planets have any effect upon life or not is immaterial in consideration and application of the system set forth in these chapters.

The influence of the Moon upon the tides and upon plant and animal life has been in considerable dispute and I believe that most of us have read many books arguing for and against such a claim. However, there are many observations which indicate that by noting the lunar cycles and the rhythm of the periods of the Moon, we cannot help coming to the conclusion that there is at least some influence measured by the periods of the Moon, which does affect animal and plant life.

Certain it is, we are able to notice a rhythmic periodicity in connection with diseases, fevers, and some normal functionings of the human body related to the psychic side of our beings, and which are coincident with the rhythmic periods of the Moon. Whether this relationship is merely incidental and of no importance, or whether it establishes and proves a great universal law, I will leave to my readers to determine. I must call attention first of all to the fact that the psychic and emotional sides of our beings are closely related to the origin, development, continuation, and final ending of all diseases, abnormal, mental, and psychological conditions, and other so-called involuntary activities of the human body.

I need not call attention to the interesting fact that has always puzzled psychologists, psychiatrists, and others, that those who are suffering from a temporary or prolonged abnormal mental condition seem to have periods of stress, quiet, action, and reaction, in keeping with the periods of the lunar rhythm. The ancients noticed this so long ago that the term *lunatic* was brought into use under the false belief that the Moon, or *luna*, was responsible for the abnormal mental states of human beings. Many of the more subtle and vital activities of the inner or secret organs of the human body are unquestionably associated with the psychic nature of humans, and also associated in some way with the lunar system.

So true is the association of the lunar rhythm with the manifestations of many of the psychic and more subtle effects and conditions of the human body that the periods of these conditions are measured by the Moon periods of approximately 28 days each.

While all this is generally admitted by the masses and by medical authorities, and undoubtedly seriously considered by the student of nature's laws, the relation of such rhythm to the phases of the Moon is not generally known. Recent discoveries by science, however, have confirmed many of the principles known to the Rosicrucians and used by them in many ways.

The Moon as a planet has a very definite cycle of phases, the cycle covering a period of approximately 28 days and known as a lunar month or a lunar cycle. We will use the term *cycle*. Because this cycle is divided into phases and these phases are also divisible, we will proceed to divide the cycle into units, each unit being a rhythmic one, as we shall see.

One half of the Moon's cycle is 14 days; one half of this (or one fourth of the cycle) is 7 days; one half of this is 3.5 days. This 3.5 days equals 84 hours.

The full cycle of the Moon constituting one complete revolution from perigree to apogee, and back again to perigee, is the lunar month referred to above. This complete cycle is often referred to as the *long cycle* of the Moon. A *short cycle*, on the other hand, would be the ordinary tide cycle corresponding to the upper and lower transits of the Moon. This short cycle is, on the average, 12 hours. Hence, we have two Moon cycles to refer to: the short one of 12 hours, known as the Moon's tide cycle, and the long one of 28 days on the average. We can deal only with averages because of slight variations in time.

Because there are long and short cycles, we will also have long and short units of these cycles. Not as an arbitrary matter, but because of fundamental laws which you will recognize, we will call the 3.5 days, arrived at above, the unit of the long cycle, or a *long unit*. Taking the short cycle of 12 hours and dividing it, we will have 3 hours as a *short unit*.

First let us note that a *long unit* of 3.5 days equals 7 short cycles, or 7 x 12 hours.

The two units, arrived at above, one of 3 hours, and one of 3.5 days, manifest themselves in the rhythmic actions of mind and body like waves or undulations of a rhythmic wave. Here is where we make important discoveries and can go beyond the findings of science, even, through our other knowledge of certain laws of nature.

In the case of diseases we find some very interesting and helpful facts by analyzing average cases and using the averages of units of the Moon's cycle. These averages betray the effect of anabolic and catabolic lunar phases or units of the cycle as shown in the incubation periods of the following diseases:

Typhoid Fever	7 - 21 days	(2 - 6 long units)
Varicella	14 days	(4 long units)
Smallpox	7 - 14 days	(2 - 4 long units)
Scarlet fever	3.5 days	(1 long unit)
Measles	10.5 days	(3 long units)
Whooping cough	10.5 days	(3 long units)
Dengue	3.5 days	(1 long unit)
Diphtheria	3.5 - 10.5 days	(1 - 3 long units)

In all acute fever cases of any name or nature the rhythmic period of these units is very pronounced and definite. Regular changes occur every seven days (as has been noted for years) or, in other words, after every two long units (one positive and one negative, as we shall see). The longer the disease continues, the more definite are the changes every seven days, and even the single unit, 3.5 days, is well marked and important.

The units of rhythm also manifest in the process of germination and gestation of life, and have the effect also of determining sex. The average time in hatching eggs of many species is 3.5 days (one long unit). In many insects it is 1.5 weeks (three long units). The hen lays eggs for three weeks (six long units) and sits on them for an equal period.

In human beings and many other forms of life each sex possesses an equal number of chromosomes, but the sex chromosomes (XX) are alike in the female and unlike in the male. The female egg contains 22 autosomes plus 1 X chromosome. The sperm are of two kinds: half of them carry 22 autosomes plus 1 X; the other half carry 22 autosomes plus 1 Y. The Y chromosomes are diminutive. When two X chromosomes come together at fertilization, the offspring is a girl. When X and Y chromosomes come together, the offspring is a boy. The difference is in potentiality or polarity.

Returning again to the short cycle of twelve hours, called the Moon's tide cycle, we find that the action of the tides gives us the key to the potentials. The six hours of time preceding the maximum point of high tide are strengthening and the six hours immediately following the hour of high tide are weakening in their effect on the psychological and psychic or emotional processes of life. The first three hours before high tide point are positive hours, or constitute a *positive short unit* (or wave) of the rhythmic cycle; while the first three hours after the point of high tide are negative and constitute the *negative short unit.* Each positive unit is preceded by a negative and followed by a negative; hence in every 12 hours, or tide cycle, there are two positive and two negative units; in each day of 24 hours there are four of each of these units. But, to be able to determine when they are negative or positive we must take the hour of high tide as the key—taking the hour of high tide as it is known for each locality on the face of the Earth, regardless of whether the locality is near a body of water or not.

Taking the long cycle or lunar month cycle of an average of 28 days, we have the long unit of 3.5 days. There are eight of these long units in each long cycle. We find that the first of these units immediately preceding the hour of full moon is a positive long unit and the unit following a full moon is a negative unit. Hence we have 3.5 days before full moon as positive in nature and 3.5 days immediately following full moon as negative in nature. There are four such positive and four such negative units of 3.5 days in each lunar cycle of 28 days.

It is easy to see that in addition to the cycles explained in previous chapters we are living under the influences of a very systematic, though strange, series of alternating psychic units of positive and negative rhythmic waves, some 3 hours long and others 3.5 days long. Therefore, while one of the long positive units of 3.5 days is in effect there will be 28 short units of 3 hours each, alternately negative and positive in effect also. A positive short unit in effect during a positive long unit will give a very positive effect; a negative short unit in effect during a positive long unit will give a neutral condition; a negative short unit in effect during a negative long unit will give a decidedly negative condition.

The long units of 3.5 days have their greatest influence on purely psychic functionings of the organs or psychic processes during disease or abnormal conditions of the body as a whole. The short units have their greatest effect on the mental, nervous, and biological functionings and processes of the body in either health or disease.

CHART C

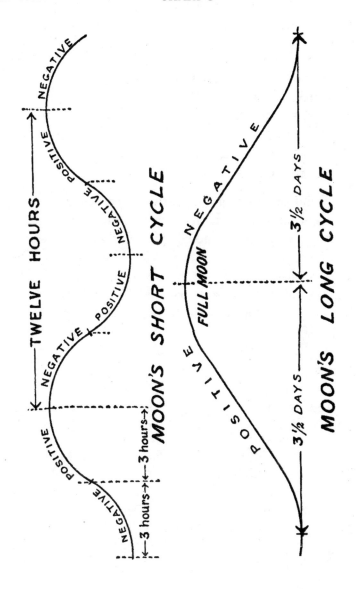

It is for this reason that the long periods have an important effect on such diseases (fevers) as we have mentioned, and many others; while in such conditions as fertilization, fecundation, contagion, and similar processes the shorter units have a greater effect. A purely positive unit or period of time produces a strong life-giving, *masculine* condition, while a purely negative unit or period produces a weaker, *feminine* condition. The one is active, the other restful. The neutral period, as mentioned above, produces a passive condition.

We find the short units exerting their influence very strongly in the conditions relating to childbirth. Here the nervous system, the sympathetic processes, and the organic functionings, are very sensitive to the influences we have been describing. During the negative long unit of time, especially *the first three hours* after high tide maximum point, the body is at rest and the contractions are weaker and less helpful during labor, while the positive long unit, especially the *first three hours immediately preceding* the high tide point, produces an active condition as far as the contractions and other process conditions are concerned, and less wilful effort is needed by the patient, with no external or artificial assistance given by the physician.

If the birth does not occur during the first two units (six hours) preceding high tide, it will not occur without forced and painful conditions during the next three hours (the first unit after high tide) or without unnecessary suffering and weakness during the next three hours (the second unit after high tide). The patient should be permitted to rest during the negative units and become active and helpful only during the first unit before high tide.

It will be noted that the contractions through labor are rhythmic and become stronger during the positive units of time and passive or weak during the negative units. By taking advantage of such influences on the rhythm the patient retains much strength, the use of drugs become unnecessary, and artificial assistance is entirely avoided. Of 100 tests made by this method, 98 confirmed each principle involved and the other two were affected by other causes and conditions of abnormality.

In thinking or planning, in talking or doing any mental or functional act that requires strength of the nervous system, impressiveness or personal magnetism and good vitality, take advantage of the positive units of time. In the treatment of disease administer all help possible during the long positive units and the short positive units, but permit the patient to rest during the negative periods. If a crisis is due during the long negative period, keep the patient as quiet as possible until a positive unit is at hand, especially a long one. Then if the patient has not succumbed, the positive unit will assist in passing over it successfully.

To properly determine the units of time one should secure from an authentic source the daily or weekly schedule of tides for the city or locality where one lives; likewise a Moon table, such as is published in most almanacs, giving the revolutions or phase and cycles of the Moon for each month.

Important Notice

All that has been learned or revealed by experiment regarding the Moon's cycles is contained in the foregoing pages of this chapter. Neither the author of the book nor the publishers can attempt to give to individual readers any information regarding the lunar periods and influence upon tides for various localities, nor the Moon's probable cycle of influence in connection with various diseases and illnesses. Whatever indefiniteness or incompleteness there may be regarding the Moon and its influence in such matters is a problem that awaits further study and investigation at the hands of the new scientific age. Let us hope that the rising generation, becoming free of the bias and prejudices of the past, will undertake this great work.

CHAPTER 11

THE DAILY CYCLES OF
SIGNIFICANT HOURS

THERE is another important cycle, which will probably be used by the readers of this book more frequently than the other cycles because of its timeliness and the ease with which it may be consulted in regard to many occurrences of the day. I know of thousands of business men and women who have used this cycle in an abbreviated form, supplied by me in the past as a guide to their affairs, and who consult it during the day in connection with every important matter that comes upon the horizon of their business or their personal affairs. We have tested this cycle in thousands of ways, and all who were fortunate enough to know of it report that it is one of the most dependable guides ever used by them.

This cycle divides the 24 hours of the day into seven periods. Each period consists of approximately 3 hours, 25 minutes, and 43 seconds. The daily cycle begins at midnight and ends at midnight; noon of each day is the center of the cycle. The first period of the cycle is from midnight to 3:25 a.m.; the second cycle ends at 6:51 a.m.; the third cycle ends at 10:17 a.m.; the fourth cycle ends at 1:42 p.m.; the fifth cycle ends at 5:08 p.m.; the sixth cycle ends at 8:34 p.m., and the seventh cycle at midnight.

These periods will apply in all parts of the world, but the time used must be the actual time of the country or the city in which the person lives. If daylight saving time is used in any locality, or any other temporary variation of clock time or standard time, as it is called, these variations must be ignored and the standard time as it is measured from Greenwich must be used.

Standard time, of course, varies slightly from mean time, but the variation is only of a few minutes in most localities, and will not require adjustment for any particular use of this cycle.

As stated in previous pages, the use of the periods of the various cycles must always allow for variations of a few minutes, hours, or days, at the beginning of each cycle. In using Cycle No. 2 and Cycle No. 3, a variation of a day, or at least of a few hours, must be allowed at the beginning and ending of each of the periods. The full effect of the conditions pertaining to each period of any of these cycles does not become manifest until the period is fairly well established.

In the case of the present cycle, no matter where you live, you should allow five minutes or even ten minutes at the beginning and ending of each period for the conditions to become established. Therefore, although the first period of this cycle ends at 3:25 in the morning, and the second one begins at that moment, it is safer to consider that the first period ends at 3:20 and the second period begins at 3:30 This leaves a neutral period of five or ten minutes at the end and beginning of each period, when the full effect of the condition allowed to the period may not be manifest. This, therefore, will take care of any slight difference between standard and mean time in your locality. Standard time is the time used by railroads, and by the government, and by it all clocks in each community are set.

The value of the daily cycles becomes apparent the minute one attempts to use the system. Testing it for a few weeks will give better warrant for its use than any argument I may present in these pages. Those who feel reluctant to guide their lives and their daily affairs by any mechanical or strange system like this need not feel that there are any superstitions connected with this matter. A superstition ceases to be a superstition as soon as the principle back of it becomes manifest, and the operation of the principle proves the existence of a fundamental law. While some may argue that the use of such systems as these is the result of faith or belief in them, the fact remains that such faith and belief are natural results from the discovery of the fact that the law is workable and *works*. As I said above, it hardly behooves me to take your time and my time to argue the benefits to be derived from this system, for it takes only a few weeks of test and trial to show the law that is in operation back of it.

Before attempting to use the daily cycle, the following chapter dealing with the complete instructions for its use must be carefully read. Once these instructions are understood, it will be a simple matter to refer to the periods of the daily cycle any hour of the day and be guided by the information given. It may be somewhat new in the lives of many persons—this regulating of their business affairs by such a schedule—but if stockbrokers and business men dealing with stocks and bonds and the fluctuations of Wall Street find it profitable to consult a system like this, and if the heads of big manufacturing and selling corporations find it helpful to consult this system in their daily affairs, certainly every business man and woman will find it pleasant, interesting, and profitable to consult the clock and the periods in this book, just as the captain of a ship consults his maps and his various guides each hour of the day and night.

CHAPTER 12

HOW TO USE THE DAILY CYCLE
OF SEVEN PERIODS

———————

A S was stated in the previous chapter, this cycle divides
the 24 hours of each day into seven periods. Each period
has approximately 3 hours and 25 minutes in it. The periods
begin at midnight and end at midnight.

Please note, however, that the periods of each day are
not identical in significance. For instance, the first period on
Sunday is quite different in significance from the first period
on Monday. And the fifth or sixth period on a Tuesday is
quite different from the fifth or sixth period on a Wednesday,
or any other day but Tuesday. All the periods of Wednesday,
for instance, are the same for every Wednesday, but they will
not apply on the other days of the week. The same thing may
be said of Thursday, Friday, or Saturday.

The charts which are given in this chapter make this very
plain and easy to understand. The illustration given herewith
of the 24-hour clock shows the day divided into A.M. and
P.M., with the seven periods of the 24 hours marked on the
dial of the clock. Please notice that midnight is at the top
of the dial and noon is at the bottom of the dial, and that
all of the hours on one side of the dial are P.M., while the
hours on the other side are A.M. This clock enables you to
see at a glance the hours in each one of the seven periods,
from midnight to midnight.

We are going to name these seven periods by the letters A, B, C, D, E, F, and G, just like the notes on a piano, or any other musical instrument. I suppose that most of my readers know that the letters of the musical scale run from A to G and begin with A again. The seven periods of the 24 hours of the day run in the same manner.

In using this daily cycle for any day of the week, merely turn to page 105 and look at Chart E (Periods for Each Day of the Week), and note what periods for the day you are to consult. Then turn to the list of daily periods and read the description which fits.

For instance: Let us suppose that it is Monday, and that you want to know what are the best things to do and what things you should avoid doing during the early business hours of Monday. By turning to Chart E, you will see that 8:00 Monday morning is in the third period of Monday; therefore, it is in Monday's "E" period, while noontime on the same day is in Monday's "F" period. By turning then to Chapter 8 and reading the description of these day periods, we look at the period for "E" and note what conditions are propitious at that time and what conditions or tendencies should be avoided. We may do the same thing for the "F" period of Monday.

Let us take another example. You may be planning to visit some person on a Monday evening around 8:00 to discuss business matters with him. By turning to Chart E you will see that 8:00 on Monday evening is in the sixth period of the day, and that it is Monday's "A" period. By referring to the description of the "A" period, you will notice that it is an excellent time in which to ask favors, and to solicit aid

CHART D

The Seven Periods of the Daily Cycle

and help from prominent persons of high positions, and so forth.

But you will also notice that this sixth period of the day ends at approximately 8:34 in the evening, and that unless you can present your proposition and get action on it before 8:34 in the evening, your discussion of it will run into the seventh period. This period, which is the "B" period of Monday, is good for visiting and social affairs and pleasantries, but not so good for the business purposes you have in mind. Therefore, your business proposition may be postponed or set aside until some other day. This warns you to try seeing your important friends earlier in the evening, but not before 5:30; that would be too early for the sixth period.

You will note, however, that although 5:30 to 8:30 is the "A" period for Monday, it is the "D" period for Tuesday, and the "G" period for Wednesday, and that if you wanted to find another good "A" period during which you might bring your business solicitation before some important persons, you would have to wait until the third period of Tuesday morning, between 7:00 and 10:00, or the "A" period of Wednesday, which would be between 8:30 p.m. and midnight.

As another illustration: Let us assume that you are anxious to find the proper period or periods of the week in which to collect some money or invest some money where it will eventually bring good returns, or you wish to start a new move or plan or proposition which you hope will be a financial success. By reading the descriptions of the day periods, you will discover that the "F" period of the daily cycle is a good one in which to do the things you are planning to do in

CHART E

PERIODS FOR EACH DAY OF THE WEEK

TIME PERIOD	SUN.	MON.	TUE.	WED.	THU.	FRI.	SAT.
No. 1 Midnight to 3:25 a.m.	G	C	F	B	E	A	D
No. 2 3:25 a.m. to 6:51 a.m.	A	D	G	C	F	B	E
No. 3 6:51 a.m. to 10:17 a.m.	B	E	A	D	G	C	F
No. 4 10:17 a.m. to 1:42 p.m.	C	F	B	E	A	D	G
No. 5 1:42 p.m. to 5:08 p.m.	D	G	C	F	B	E	A
No. 6 5:08 p.m. to 8:34 p.m.	E	A	D	G	C	F	B
No. 7 8:34 p.m. to Midnight	F	B	E	A	D	G	C

connection with financial matters. Now, by consulting Chart E you will note that there are seven "F" periods in the week.

The first one is during the seventh period of Sunday from 8:34 to 12:00 p.m.; the next one is during the fourth period of Monday, which is from 10:17 a.m. to 1:42 p.m.; the next one is in the first period of Tuesday morning, midnight to 3:25; the next one is in the fifth period of Wednesday, from 1:42 p.m. to 5:08 p.m.; the next one is the second period of Thursday, which is from 3:25 a.m. to 6:51 in the morning; the next one is during the sixth period of Friday, which is from 5:08 p.m. to 8:34 p.m.; and the last one is during the third period of Saturday, which is from 6:51 a.m. to 10:17 a.m.

In picking out the best of the seven "F" periods, or any other of the lettered periods of the week, two points should be kept in mind. First, those that are late at night or very early in the morning must be eliminated because of the impossibility of using these midnight hours for general purposes. Second, one should be guided by the best periods for the particular thing to be accomplished, bearing in mind that several of these lettered periods may serve the purpose, rather than only one. In the illustration just given above, of the "F" periods, we find there are seven that you can use for your financial purposes, and of these seven, the best ones to use would be the "F" period of Monday, which is during the early business hours of the morning, or the "F" period of Wednesday, which is early afternoon, or the "F" period of Friday, which is between 5:00 and 8:00 p.m.

The next important way in which to use these daily periods is as follows: Suppose that someone comes to you with a business proposition, a plan, a request, a demand, or a suggestion of some kind, and you find yourself becoming interested in what is proposed or required. Before taking any action on the matter, you should immediately turn to the description of these daily periods and to the table of these and see what period of the day you are in, and note whether it is a propitious time for the matter in hand.

Let us say that the person who has come to you has a contract or an agreement, or a lease, or some paper to sign, and glowing terms and promises are being expressed to you, and you have been swayed by oratory, fine words, and fine arguments. Suppose that when you turn to the charts in these pages, you find that this matter has come before you on a Monday morning, at 9:30. You find that this is an "E" period for Monday, and not a good period for signing papers, signing contracts or agreements, and not a good period in which to place any faith in the spoken promises and glittering word pictures of anyone. In this way you will be warned not to enter into the matter but to dismiss it.

Even if you attempt to hold the matter off until the next period, which is an "F" period, and therefore fortunate for financial matters and for contracts and papers, you will not help matters, since the matter actually had its birth and its start in your interests during the "E" period. By your voluntary postponement of it, you will not help yourself, for that would be establishing an artificial condition. If, on the other hand, the person who proposed these things to you had come to you during the "F" period instead of the "E" period, you could have felt that it was safer and more dependable.

On the other hand, suppose that these matters had been presented to you by this man on Friday at the same hour, 11:30. By reference to the description of the lettered periods of the day, you would find that this "D" period of Friday at 11:30 is not a good time for the making of agreements, contracts, or investments that are to last for any length of time or have any degree of permanency to them; therefore, you would refuse to enter into the proposition and would dismiss it.

Bear in mind that once a matter is dismissed by you or dropped by you because it has come to you in a period that indicates that it is not safe or good, it should never be taken up again at any other period. To attempt to do this would be to frustrate the principles of this system, and set them aside entirely. If a proposition comes to you at a period that indicates that it is not a good thing for you to enter into, its merits will not be changed by having it come up again at another period. One cannot imagine a mining proposition that is thoroughly unsound, or a speculative business proposition that has no foundation to it, being radically changed and made safe and sound overnight by delaying the presentation of the proposition a few hours.

The significance lies in the period in which it comes to you for the first time. A proposition may be perfectly safe for others to invest in or to consider or cooperate with, but for you, it is not safe, or good, or propitious, or fortunate, and this is signified by the time in which it first comes to your attention. Therefore, you will be justified in setting it aside permanently, even though others who hear of it at a more propitious time may find it good for them and go into it. If you are to get any benefit out of this system at all, it must be remembered that the system in each application is representing you, and your best interests, and not all humanity.

A person may come to your home or to your business office, with some proposition, at 10:00 in the morning, and because of the hour and the period, you find it advisable to reject it as being unfavorable or unfortunate. The solicitor, however, may walk a few blocks and present the same proposition to one of your neighbors. During the time of his walk, the third period of the day has ended, and the fourth period has begun, and so the solicitor approaches your neighbor in an entirely different period than the one in which he approached you, and the fourth period may be a propitious or fortunate time for the proposition he submits. Therefore, your neighbor would be warranted in accepting it, whereas you rejected it.

This does not show a weakness or an inconsistency in the system. We all know that there are propositions which are fortunate, helpful, and worthy of consideration on the part of some persons, while the same things are unfortunate and inadvisable for other persons. We know that one man can invest money in a certain proposition and make money out of it, while others who invest in it realize later that it was not a fortunate thing for them. This system, therefore, is consistent with the varied conditions which surround each individual, and helps to explain why there are such inequalities and unequal opportunities and advantages for human beings.

By carefully studying and analyzing the matters set forth in Chapter 13, describing the lettered periods of the day, you will become familiar with those things which should be undertaken, planned, or started and those things which should be avoided or dismissed during the different periods. Therefore, you should watch the hours of each day in your office, business, or home affairs, and act accordingly.

Perhaps one interesting point should be emphasized here. It appears from a long test of this system by persons who have kept accurate statistics and records of the results, that the more urgent the proposition which a person is considering, and the more vital it is to his personal or business affairs, the more important it is to him to consider the period and act accordingly. In other words, the more trivial affairs of social and business life, or the mere routine matters of daily business and social affairs may be carried on safely without consulting this system.

But to the same degree that any matter is of vital moment and calls for careful judgment, careful analysis, and considerable thought, an intense consideration should be given the system and the period of the day. Surely in any matter that is of utmost importance, where the decision or choice will bring lasting and serious results for either good or bad, it is far better to consult this system and be guided by it than to depend upon hasty judgment, a toss of the coin, or the acceptance of an urge that may be a temptation and an external suggestion from some other mind.

As has been stated in an earlier chapter of this book, urges, inspirations, temptations, and impulses to do things or to hesitate in doing things come to us from the Cosmic and from the minds of persons around us, and very often there are two impulses or two urges, two arguments, two tendencies, and we must choose between them and accept one or the other. Here is where we exert our privilege as a free agent, but we must ever abide by the result of our decision. It is far better, therefore, to place dependence in a system like this than in our objective analytical ability, or in any rational system of thinking or superficial analysis.

This system has been tried and tested and proved to be in accordance with some higher laws that you may not understand, or which may not even interest you. Yet here is the system, and its simplicity, wide range of adaptability and power to beget confidence, warrants its use. You can make of it a real silent partner in all your personal, private, or public affairs.

WITH THE CYCLES OF LIFE

DESCRIPTION OF DAILY PERIODS

"A" PERIOD

THERE are many things which may be done during this period of the day, with the hope of fortunate realization and cosmic cooperation. For instance, one may concentrate or meditate upon any plan for the purpose of evolving its details; he may ask favors from persons in high positions, especially when such favors relate to a promotion in position, in political power, or in social position; he may ask for stays or delays in legal procedure, the loan of money, the endorsement or recommendation of a proposition, the introduction to a person in high position.

This is a propitious time for dealing with public officials, or persons of high rank; the signing of wills, deeds, or transfers, the writing of important letters that seek favors, promotions, or recommendations, or which carry to the mind of another person a high regard of one's self, his business, or any plan he is proposing. It is a good time in which to talk to bankers or financiers for the purpose of building up personal credit or the credit of a business, the making of a public appearance or address for the purpose of bringing esteem and honor to yourself or your business, or for building up your reputation or the reputation of your affairs.

It is not a good period to deal with criminals or evil matters, even as a lawyer or adviser. It is a time filled with energy which must be controlled. It is also a period filled with fiery impulses which must be governed, just as all words and acts must be cautiously controlled. It is not a good period to start a new business, a new plan, or a new proposition of any kind; it is not good for the buying of livestock; neither is it good for the signing of contracts or agreements.

It is not a good period in which to start short journeys of several days' duration, nor is it a good period in which to deal with marital affairs or to marry, or to go courting. It is a bad period in which to loan money, to move into a new location for either home or business, or to start the erection of a new building of any kind. And it is not a good time in which to make the first financial investment in a new business. It is not fortunate for buying real estate or even for selling or renting it. Nor is it a good period for surgical operations.

"B" PERIOD

This period is fortunate for the following things: Matters dealing with art, music, the beautifying of the home or person, or with matters pertaining to purely material and sensual affairs. It is an excellent period for starting any new undertaking; for the enjoyment of art, music, and drama; for the buying of livestock; for the collecting of accounts; or for dealing with the public in connection with public administration, public affairs, and public utilities, or soliciting business from the public. It is also good for the hiring of agents, collectors, traveling representatives, salesmen, and employees for important positions in the business or home.

New acquaintances made during this period are generally dependable and worthy of friendship and trust, if they come into your life purely in a social way. It is a good period to start short journeys, lasting for two or three days, or less than a month; a good time for marriage and courting, for loaning money or borrowing money; to put into material form any new plans for business or pleasure; for indulging in recreation and social function. It is also a good period for seeking favors in a social way, or business favors in social circles. It is also good for speculating, for games of chance, and for investments of a speculative nature; also a good period for dealing with women in either business or social matters.

It is not a period of great ambition, and while it is changeable, it is easily adapted to many conditions. It is a fruitful period inasmuch as most things started or culminated during this period will be more prolific than one may anticipate. It also brings its impulses of an intellectual and social nature, which must be guarded against. It is not a good time for hiring servants or persons for menial positions, and is not a good time for starting long journeys, especially those which either by train or water take one far from home.

"C" PERIOD

This period is especially fortunate for dealing with the fine arts, or the intellectual things of life, especially education, scientific research, publishing, printing, instructing in schools, colleges, universities, and in the promotion of campaigns involving an educational element. It is a good time for study, memory work, and absorption of special knowledge, analytical examination of documents, books, papers, and propositions, or to deal with legal arguments in court requiring the use of the intellect and logic. It is an especially good period for mental activity of any kind, including writing, thinking, speaking, and self-examination. It is also a good period to indulge in the drama, music, and art.

The buying of livestock, or dealing in cattle or the livestock market, is fortunate during this period. It is a good time for the making of contracts providing same are not for long periods but of short duration, collecting of accounts, making of new acquaintances that are dependable, the hiring of business employees and servants of all kinds and classes. It is also a good time to start short journeys, to do literary and newspaper work, prepare advertising, start new advertising campaigns, or to send out literature to the public pertaining to business or social affairs.

It is also a fortunate time for the taking of medicine or any system of therapeutics which is to benefit the physical body. It is a good time to lend money, but it is questionable whether it is a good period in which to borrow. It is a good time in which to erect new buildings, or to plan new undertakings; and students of the occult, the philosophical, and metaphysical will find that this is an excellent period for study and objective realization of great truths.

It is a good period in which to take a chance with undertakings that are highly tricky, or questionable from a financial point of view, for one who has the means to do this without bringing financial embarrassment should the result not be all that is expected. It is a good period in which to have a few minutes of recreation or social intercourse, and for signing important papers of all kinds, and it is likewise the best period for traveling salesmen to call upon the most difficult of prospective customers. It is also a good time for writing important letters.

This period is not good for dealing with private or public enemies or bringing them into court, or attempting to adjust matters with them, for this period will bring endless discussions and arguments without any beneficial results. It is a period that is quite changeable in many ways, giving great mental activity, but is not good for prudence and caution, and, therefore, no dependence should be placed in one's usual cautiousness. It is not good for marriage, and it is a questionable period to deal with lawyers in regard to any problem, or to deal with inventions and mechanical problems, or to seek promotion in business, or to ask for the favor or recognition of public officials or prominent persons. It is not a good time to buy real estate, and it is questionable whether it is a good time to sell real estate. It is a doubtful period for seeking favors, or for spiritual development or concentration, and is a very unfortunate period for dealing with surgeons or having a surgical operation of any kind.

It should be remembered that during this period one comes in contact with the nimbleness of mind and tongue. Any person presenting a proposition or plan to you at this time is very apt to exaggerate or mislead through his statements or his evidence. Forgers, blackmailers, and persons who are deceitful, lying, and too nimble with their expert fingers, are apt to present themselves during this period. Therefore guard yourself accordingly.

"D" PERIOD

Here we have a period that is especially fortunate for all general material affairs of business, dealings with the public in any general capacity, educational work of any kind, planting or farming operations, the making of new acquaintances, and the hiring of servants of all classes.

It is also a good period in which to start short journeys or long journeys by water, and for writing, supervising, or dealing with literary or newspaper work. It is also a good period for marriage or for courting, for all marine affairs, for the taking of medicine or any system of therapeutic help for the body or mind, for metaphysical study and analysis, or for dealing with shipping interests, transportation interests, or the actual shipping of goods to places out of the city in which you may live. It is also good for dealing with surgeons or for surgical operations, and it is one of the good periods for salesmen, traveling agents, and others to solicit and sell, and for dealing especially with women. It is a period in which the ambitions may be highly aroused, and while these ambitions may be very impulsive, they will generally prove fruitful.

It is not a good period for commencing any new undertaking, the buying of livestock, the making of contracts, or the signing of legal papers of any kind, or starting lawsuits or court actions. It is not a good period in which to borrow money or attempt to borrow it, nor sign any papers or notes pertaining to money matters, nor speculate, nor take part in games of chance of any kind. It is also a bad period for writing letters, pleas, or requests of any kind asking for important favors or aids in connection with business, personal, or social life.

"E" PERIOD

This period is particularly good for aggressive pursuits, or those activities that require deep thought followed by a long campaign or a long period of steady action. It is good to begin these things during this period. It is an excellent time to have one's affairs come before judges, referees, magistrates, police authorities, senators, governors, mayors, or the presidents of large corporations, or those persons who have within their power the privilege to decide or render decisions in any matters of dispute. It is a good period for bringing permanency to anything started or finished during it, and gives great persistency and endurance to all activities.

It is also good for literary or newspaper work or advertising, or sales promotion by mail through the use of letters or brief printed communications. It is good, too, for starting any legal action in court, or for the submission of briefs or arguments, and for all inventions or mechanical problems or matters dealing with them, also for matters pertaining to metallurgy, or affairs with metal workers. It is a good time to move into a new house or to buy and sell real estate or to move into or transfer real estate. It is an excellent period for starting or indulging in scientific pursuits, and for spiritual meditation.

This period, however, is also unfortunate for certain things, and these are quite definite; it should be noted that the unfortunate things will prove to be unfortunate indeed. They are: The making of contracts or agreements of any kind, other than the purchase of homes; attempting to collect money; the planting of seeds, or starting of farm operations; making new acquaintances for the first time; the hiring of servants, agents, salesmen, or collectors of any class or for any position.

The period is also very unfortunate for starting long journeys especially by water; for marriage; the taking of medicine or any method of mental or physical cure; borrowing or loaning money; erecting new buildings; dealing with public officials or prominent persons from whom you seek personal favors or special recognition; starting any risky business; indulging in recreational or social affairs; speculating in business, in the stock market, or otherwise; being operated upon by a surgeon; or for writing letters of an important nature.

"F" PERIOD

This is one of the most fortunate periods in each day. It might be called the lucky period, just as the preceding one is generally considered the unlucky period. During this period of each day, we find conditions are fortunate for the starting of any new undertaking, such as the buying or marketing of cattle or livestock, either in speculation or for actual business purposes; for making contracts or signing contracts, agreements, and all papers of specific stipulation; for collecting accounts or raising money; for educational work and educational interests; or for making new acquaintances.

It is also a good period for starting long journeys, either for business or pleasure, and also for short journeys by water and other means, and for literary and newspaper work, or for dealing with lawyers, or the submission of briefs of papers to court, or the actual starting of court procedure. It is also good for marriage or courting, for borrowing money, erecting of new buildings, working out the plans of new undertakings, and holding directors' meetings for the discussion of business conditions or new ventures, for seeking promotion in business, or the building up of trade and credit reputes, dealing with public officials, or with the public mass in all affairs, or with prominent persons. It is a good time for the buying or selling of real estate, for all social affairs and recreations, for seeking favors and for signing papers dealing with important matters of any nature. It is the fortunate period for all forms of speculation, and for the writing of important letters.

There are a few things that should be noticed in regard to this fortunate period, however. It is a period that brings a great deal of energy to the body and mind, and tempts one to overdraw in many ways. And yet with all the impulsiveness of this period it is generally fruitful, and, therefore, fortunate. It is a more fortunate period for men than for women in business affairs, but more fortunate for women than men in social affairs. It is a period of positiveness, and yet with a natural tendency toward caution and prudence. It generally gives and begets the spirit and love of justice, and the period makes for permanency. It is not a good time for hiring servants for any menial position, nor is it good for marine affairs.

"G" PERIOD

This period is especially good for mastering those affairs which require considerable energy and aggressiveness, endurance, and persistency. It is an excellent period for dealing with those matters that require the expenditure of more physical energy than mental energy, and require real labor and muscle. Therefore, all material and sensual affairs will be fortunate during this period, as well as the collecting of money, the hiring of traveling salesmen, agents or collectors, or the soliciting on their part. It is also fortunate for martial affairs, marine affairs, the working out of mechanical problems, inventions, or building plans, or matters dealing with metal and metal workers. It is also good for scientific pursuits.

It is not a good period for any beneficent matters, or matters dealing with the receipt of gifts or favors, or public humanitarian activities, nor is this period fraught with much prudence and caution. It is an unfortunate period for the buying of cattle or livestock, or speculating with them, or for dealing with enemies, or for starting long journeys, or for legal actions, or dealings with lawyers or matters in court. Naturally it would be a bad period for marriage or for courting, and for seeking favors generally. It is very questionable whether it is a good period for surgical operations, or for dealing with women. This is the period in which accidents are apt to occur; therefore, one should be careful about being in any place of hazard or being near firearms, fire explosions, or other things that would affect the physical body. In illness, fevers are apt to be high during this time and the temperature of the body is naturally warmer during this period than at any other.

SELF-MASTERY AND FATE

CHAPTER 14

THE SOUL CYCLE

IN preceding chapters we have spoken of the cosmic vibrations and emanations throughout the universe, and the effect that these have upon the personal affairs of human beings through the tendencies, urges, inspirations, and conditions they create or stimulate in our daily lives. It should be apparent to anyone who analyzes the principles involved that these cosmic vibrations and cosmic periods of rhythm would have some effect upon the soul, personality, and character of each human being.

As was stated before, the ideas contained in this book and the various systems presented herewith have no relationship with the postulations and principles of the so-called art of astrology. However, if the soul entering each human body at birth is an essential part of the cosmic energy or cosmic vitality and if this energy or vitality reaches the Earth's surface in rhythmic pulsations of various combinations of rates and resulting tendencies, then a person born at any rhythmic period of the year should have natural tendencies different from those possessed by a person born during a different rhythmic period. It is not my intention to enter into a scientific explanation of how this is so, and why, but merely to present the effects of such rhythmic pulsations upon the soul and character of classes of individuals, and let these facts establish the existence of the law. Those who wish to devote their time and study to a deep investigation of the principles involved may do so, and they will find in the work much knowledge and happiness.

Passing over the laws or principles, therefore, we come to the *observed facts,* and note that the *solar year* of 365 days may be divided into seven distinct periods, which constitute the *soul cycle.*

It must be borne in mind that the solar year begins on or about March 22, when we have that distinct astro-phenomenon known as the *spring equinox.* In all countries, as in ancient times, the birth of the new year occurs on or about March 22. The establishment of January 1 as the beginning of a new year is a purely arbitrary thing and has no foundation in natural law. The solar year is approximately 365 days in length, and for all general purposes we may figure the year as being 365 days long. If divided into seven equal periods, we find that once again we have a periodicity of 52 days and a few hours. We may ignore the fraction of a day in each period, and make each period an even 52 days, as we have with the other cycles.

Therefore, we begin the soul cycle on March 22, and divide it into periods of 52 days each as follows: From March 22 to May 12; May 13 to July 3; July 4 to August 24; August 25 to October 15; October 16 to December 6; December 7 to January 27; January 28 to March 21. Each of these periods has a dual polarity, and we find that the first half of each period produces a slightly different effect from the last half of each period. Therefore, we have seven periods, each having two natures, and producing a total of fourteen distinct natures or combinations of conditions.

Now everyone who is born takes the first breath of life and breathes into his system that cosmic energy which starts his soul consciousness in attunement with the cosmic vibrations and rhythm existing at that time, and, according to the ancient observations which have been verified through centuries of careful examination and scrutiny, each person *continues to vibrate in attunement with the rhythm established at the moment of birth.* It is as though each person becomes an affinity of the rhythmic conditions existing at the time of birth, and, therefore, is continuously more sensitive, receptive, and responsive to the effects of that rhythm than to any of the others. It is as though various notes on a perfectly tuned musical instrument were being played at different hours of the day, and that a person who was born just as the note "A" was being played would ever after be responsive to and affected by the sound of "A" or the vibrations of the note "A" to a greater degree than to any of the other notes played in the entire octave.

As a matter of fact, we are, as individuals, attuned to certain musical notes or musical rates of vibrations, and that is why some pieces of music which have our natural note more predominant than other notes affect us strongly. Every created material thing has its musical note, whether it be a glass pitcher or goblet, a chair, a mechanical device, or a copper pot. The note with which it is attuned is its natural note, and, therefore, there are certain harmonics of this note which have effects upon it also, to a lesser extent and in a different manner. If a harmonic of the true natural note of a glass vessel can be properly played upon a violin string, for instance, it may either cause the glass vessel to shatter to pieces, or it may have some other effect upon it, according to which harmonic of the natural note is played. All of this, however, deals with other principles than those covered in the present volume, and may some day be presented in another volume dealing with natural harmonics in human life.

In outlining the system of the soul cycle, we observe that the seven periods with two polarities to each of them give us fourteen combinations of notes or rhythmic pulsations which produce certain definite characteristics, tendencies, and elements in the personality or *soul consciousness* of each individual. It is my purpose to outline each of the fourteen periods, so that the reader may have a true character analysis of the *inner nature* or *soul personality* of every person he contacts.

Before beginning to outline this system, with the various descriptions, I must call the reader's attention to the following important points. It must be kept in mind that the cosmic effect upon the *soul consciousness* of each person does not always manifest itself in the *outer, objective nature* of an individual. The inner personality of people we meet may be very different from the outer individuality or character. In many cases only intimate, friendly relationships over a long period of time will reveal to us the true inner nature of a person whom we think we have understood very thoroughly.

The outer, objective mind and character of a person may clothe him with certain tendencies, habits, expressions, and mannerisms which he may have assumed or acquired, or even affected for various reasons, and which may not be truly consistent with the inner self. The various systems of character reading, such as palmistry, physiognomy, phrenology, handwriting, and so forth may be a fair index to the characteristics of the outer self, with occasional points relating to the inner self, but all of those systems fail in giving us a true picture of the inherent, deep-seated *soul personality.*

Very often we find through character analysis of the outer self that persons whom we meet are in different occupations, professions, avocations, or social positions than we expected or anticipated to find them. We discover, then, that the system we had used for such character reading was only an index to the changing objective self, and because this outer self is vacillating and has the power and privilege to assume and affect *temporary* conditions, mannerisms, choices of professions and occupations, that we can place no dependability upon the system we have used. Whenever we use the system, however, that gives us an index of the *inner nature* of any person, we find upon close questioning and intimate association that, regardless of the outer life and characteristics of the person, inwardly, privately, and in seclusion these persons live true to the inner index and cosmic soul nature.

Furthermore, it avails us very little to become thoroughly acquainted with the outer character and nature of any individual. As far as any benefit being derived from a knowledge of the outer nature of a person is concerned, it is just as safe and serves just as much purpose to take persons as we find them outwardly and casually. Very few persons are capable of concealing their true outward natures. An acquaintance-ship with anyone for one day, which would include casual conversation with him and an observation of his activities in business or home life, will tell us as much about his outer habits and outer characteristics as any involved system that has ever been devised. I mean, of course, that to the student of human nature and to the analytical mind this would be so.

Knowing the general outer, objective, material traits, habits, and characteristics of a person does not in any considerable way give us an advantage, benefit, or protection. The man who is a thief outwardly and in all of his habits cannot conceal that from the careful observer. It is the man who is inwardly a thief, cheat, and deceiver, while outwardly posing as honest, dependable and reliable, that must be guarded against, and against whom we must be protected and warned.

In all social and business relations, the real value of character analysis or intimate acquaintance with personality must relate to the *true self within*, and not to the fictitious, temporary, vacillating, inconsequential outer self. If we would know whether it is safe to trust another person with our secrets, money, confidence, or association, then we must know the real nature and personality within, regardless of the artificial or temporary characteristics of the outer self. If we would know whom to select for a partner in business or marriage, whom to select as a friend or companion, or to perform an important errand or commission, or to fill an important position or place of authority, we must judge by the true inner nature and not by the temporary nature of the outer self.

If we would know our friends better, and understand their moods with the resulting fancies, foibles, and tendencies, we must know the real inner selves of those friends and disregard the outer selves.

If parents want to understand their children and help them to develop along the lines that originated as natural cosmic tendencies, and which will keep them in attunement with the cosmic personalities born within them, and result in greater happiness and success in life, the parents should have an intimate understanding of the *inner natures of the children,* and disregard the passing characteristics that impinge themselves upon children as a result of casual association, imitation of another's habits, and similar external influences of a temporary nature.

And above all else, if we would know our real self and learn *why* there seems to be a constant conflict between the changing desires and wishes of the outer self, and the natural tendencies that urge from within, and thereby make the best of our life in all affairs and in every situation, we should know with what tendencies, abilities, characteristics, and strong points of personality we are born, and thereby become acquainted with the inner self in a surprising manner.

The following index to *soul character and personality* will do all these things in a different manner than any system of character reading has ever done heretofore. But just because the indications and index of characteristics given herewith pertain to the inner self, the reader must be warned against what may seem to him to be contradictions or inconsistencies.

You may be tempted to use your own life as the first example with which to test this system. You may select your birthday from the table of periods published herewith and discover in what period and what polarity of the period of the solar year you were born. Then turning to the descriptive index for that period, you may read that you have characteristics, tendencies, faculties, and abilities that seem different from those that you have been using, manifesting, and exhibiting outwardly to yourself and to your closest acquaintances.

Here, then, will be the temptation for you to feel that this system is either unreliable or incomplete. You may say to yourself, or to others, that you do not have the tendencies and characteristics indicated in these pages. The experts who have used this system, however, would say to you, "How do you know whether these are your real, inner characteristics or not?" You may say that you have often thought of yourself, noticed your natural habits, and carefully analyzed your inner wishes and desires. But the expert will say to you that until you have carefully analyzed yourself over a period of many years, and have carefully tabulated, without bias, prejudice, or personal interest, the strong and weak points of your character, *you cannot be a proper judge* of the real nature that was born into you at the time of your birth.

You will find that you will do better in testing the system to read the inner characteristics and nature of *someone with whom you have been acquainted* over a long period, and with a few of whose inner, personal traits you have become acquainted. If you are able to judge the other person without personal interest, and without personal bias or prejudice, you will be able to discern his subtle and minute traits of inner character better than you are able to judge your own.

The real value of this index is that it enables the honest investigator of his own inner self, or of the inner selves of his children and friends, to help strengthen the inherited birthrights that are good, and overcome those which are unfortunate or undesirable. In other words, this index should become a guide to character building, and the molding of a more ideal and perfect personality.

Granting that each one of us is born with certain tendencies, with certain natural abilities and special faculties, it is certain that the best of these, or those which are good and useful, will become a greater asset to us if developed than any abilities or capabilities which we may arbitrarily assume to be ours, and artificially create in our own lives.

Let us say, for example, that a man's inner nature is revealed in the index as being that of a natural healer or *physician*, and that he has certain cosmic tendencies and abilities for healing which, although part of his inner nature, remain dormant awaiting development, application, and usefulness. Let us assume also that not knowing of this natural tendency of his inner nature, he arbitrarily selected as his profession that of architecture, because of acquaintances he had in that profession, and because of another inner, natural tendency toward art and drawing.

To become the proficient architect that he wishes to be, he has to create and build up a faculty or ability that was not naturally born in him, and this effort requires years of study, along with years of patient practice. Even so, he cannot attain in his profession of architecture that success, prosperity, and renown which would come to him if he had become a physician. He would find that to become a proficient physician he would have had to do less studying, less concentration upon the development of his ability, and less striving after the success and fame that he sought.

As an architect, he might attain a reputation as a careful, conscientious, and mechanically exact worker. As a physician, however, he would have attained the reputation for being an inspired, natural, prolific, and wonderful healer. There would be that difference between his work as a physician and his work as an architect that is noticeable in the work of the great masters in art, music, and the sciences, which comes from inner inspiration and so-called fortunate inheritance.

Another person may have an inner, natural ability for writing and for the beautiful expression of thoughts in impressive language. Not conscious of this natural tendency, he may become a painter or a musician by arbitrary choice, or because within him there was also the cosmic urge to express himself in the finer arts. To become a proficient musician or painter would require for him many years of study and practice, accompanied by many years of suffering and privation, bringing fame and fortune to his name only after he had passed to the great Beyond.

As a writer, however, he would have found his pen and mind becoming more facile and prolific in expression, with less study and less practice than art required, and he would have found fame and fortune early in his life and would have lived to enjoy the fruits of his divine inheritance. As a writer, he would have been recognized as an inspired thinker, but as an artist or musician he would have been classified as mediocre, or perhaps simply as a successful one who had battled against the odds of life to attain recognition.

In other words, the faculties and tendencies which are our divine inheritance through cosmic direction at the time of birth are the things which we may easily develop and apply in our lives to attain success, happiness, prosperity, and at the same time contribute to the needs of humanity and the benefits of civilization.

It would appear, therefore, from all of the observable facts, that each one of us is born to fulfill certain niches in life and to carry on definite missions in connection with certain lines of work in our earthly lives. We hear so often of the *born* musician, the *born* artist, the *born* business man, the *born* creator and thinker, and others, who seem to have come into this life with certain abilities well established and well developed. Such persons are those who have learned, or discovered in some way, their true inheritance and natural birthright, and have been permitted to develop along these inherited lines and to become successful in expressing them for the benefit of others.

A musician may be born in a family of carpenters, and a great architect may be born in a family of farmers who have never had even a primitive realization of architectural design. A great musician may be born in a family of persons who have never heard good music and had no opportunity of judging between good music and that which is otherwise. Nothing can explain this great diversity of natural tendencies, except the cosmic law of divine inheritance. That in some cases a carpenter may have a son who becomes even more successful than himself in that trade, or an artist or musician may have a son or daughter who follows successfully in the same line, in no wise warrants the belief that physical inheritance determines the natural tendencies and attributes which we find in all human beings.

Therefore, in the following chapters a complete system is offered to you whereby you may analyze and study the inner, natural, inherited tendencies, abilities, and traits of character of any man, woman, or child. Again the note of warning must be sounded in regard to the differences in the stages of evolution to be found in the human race.

It has been proven that there is truly no racial supremacy. Those of any race given equal opportunity and advantage will display in one or more generations an intelligence equal to any other. This has been shown in the case of individuals whose parents and grandparents lived under the most primitive conditions. When the offspring were reared in a higher civilization and given an advanced education, they attained success in intellectual capacities.

Remarkable accomplishments, however, on the part of what once were erroneously called inferior races, when given the opportunity to develop their natural tendencies, plainly indicate that neither race nor color have any bearing upon the blessings which each human being may receive from the Cosmic. And this should make all of us more tolerant and sympathetic in our thought of those in other lands, and among other races, who may not have the advantages we may have, but are nevertheless equal with us as sons of God and recipients of the cosmic benedictions.

CHAPTER 15

HOW TO DETERMINE THE PERIODS OF THE SOUL CYCLE

IN the following pages you will find an outline of the seven periods of the soul cycle for the solar year. Every person's birthday comes within one of these seven periods. You will also note that each of the seven periods is divided into two polarities, an A and B polarity.

For instance, the first period in the soul cycle is from March 22 to May 12. This period is subdivided into two polarities: the A polarity from March 22 to April 17, and the B polarity from April 17 to May 12. A person born on April 20 would be in the B polarity of the first period of the soul cycle. A person born on December 3 would be in the B polarity of the fifth period of the soul cycle. A person born on March 21 would be in the B polarity of the seventh soul cycle.

Persons who are born at midnight on the division of any period will have to be judged by a combination of the indications given for both periods. For instance, a person who was born at midnight on October 15 would have his birthday on the precise division between the fourth and fifth periods of the cycle. Therefore, to judge the inner character of this person, a blending of the B polarity of the fourth cycle and the A polarity of the fifth cycle would have to be taken into consideration. All of the seven periods end at midnight and begin at midnight of the days indicated, and the same is true of the A and B polarities. A person born at midnight on June 8 would be in the second period of the cycle, but in reading the description of the character and personality, a blending of both the A and B polarities of the second period would have to be taken into consideration.

The hour of birth has naught to do with this system, except as it pertains to the midnight hour as stated above. The *place* of birth has naught to do with this system, unless the birth occurred years ago in some country like Russia, where the calendar has been changed and the true day of birth is not definitely known. The *year of birth* is of no importance, for the periods in the cycle are the same year after year. It is better not to attempt to analyze the characteristics or personality of a person when the precise birthdate is not known, unless, of course, it is known to be within two or three days of the center of one of the polarities of the periods, when a variation of a few days will not make any particular difference.

Perhaps one other little word of advice or recommendation may be accepted by you. Personally, I would appreciate it if all those who are using this system and who may, from time to time, copy from this book a description of some person and give it to him as a helpful guide, would when doing this, call the written description not a life reading or a horoscope, or any similar term that may be misleading, but a *Soul Reading from the Cycles of Life.*

This will distinguish these descriptions from so-called life readings or astrological readings with which they have no connection, and with which they should not be related

CHART F

PERIODS AND POLARITIES OF THE SOUL CYCLE

Period No. 1   March 22 - May 12
        Polarity A   March 22 - April 17
        Polarity B   April 17 - May 12

Period No. 2   May 13 - July 4
        Polarity A   May 13 - June 8
        Polarity B   June 8 - July 3

Period No. 3   July 4 - August 24
        Polarity A   July 4 - July 31
        Polarity B   July 31 - August 24

Period No. 4   August 25 - October 15
        Polarity A   August 25 - September 20
        Polarity B   September 20 - October 15

Period No. 5   October 16 - December 6
        Polarity A   October 16 - November 11
        Polarity B   November 11 - December 6

Period No. 6   December 7 - January 27
        Polarity A   December 7 - January 1
        Polarity B   January 1 - January 27

Period No. 7   January 28 - March 21
        Polarity A   January 28 - February 23
        Polarity B   February 23 - March 21

even in the mind of a person who is not familiar with any of these systems. It is the wish of the author to keep the systems in this book distinguished from all others, as they have been in his own personal use for so many years. You will find generally that your friends and acquaintances will appreciate the knowledge that the reading or description you give them is from a different system, and resulting from a unique method that is free from any superstitious beliefs or any principles that may be undesirable in their minds.

CHAPTER 16

DESCRIPTION OF THE PERIODS OF THE SOUL CYCLE

PERIOD NO. 1
March 22 to May 12

THOSE in this period inherit from the Cosmic a very lofty nature, with a deep-seated desire to achieve a high place or a high position in the esteem of the public and in the hearts of their closest acquaintances. They carry over from their previous incarnations the lessons and tribulations which have taught them the necessity for looking above and beyond the commonplace things of life and holding a vision of the highest ideals as their goals. They also carry into this life recollections of the experience of having achieved a notable place or position in life in some foreign land, and having tasted of a full cup with many of the luxurious and beautiful things of earthly existence.

Therefore, in this incarnation, no matter in what station socially, racially, or financially they may be, there is always the inner urge to try to live a noble life, or at least one that will be above the commonplace, and that will bring them the respect and perhaps the adoration of the multitude. There is not just the desire for wealth, or the material luxuries of life, although there is a taste for these things slightly beyond the average; but the great desire, the great longing, that actuates these persons in their subjective thinking and planning is the attainment of public renown and approval.

For this reason, these persons reluctantly deal with sordid things and constantly struggle against things that are mean, lowly, or objectionable to good taste and high ethical standards. This means that if these persons are starting this incarnation or the lessons of this life in a lowly social or financial position, there is a continual restlessness and dissatisfaction that urges them onward and upward. They always sense the nobility of their last life. They are generally trustworthy, for they have learned in the past that deceit, falsity, underhandedness, and unethical practices hold them back in the progress they wish to make. Their words are generally their bonds, and their aspirations are not dreamy or mystical, but practical, and adhere to a straight line of progress.

There is, of course, the natural tendency carried over from the past to want to rule and dominate, and, therefore, be the heads or be the leaders of any plan, organization, or group of interests with which they may be connected, and in such capacities they will succeed because of the other inherent qualities. They are generally careful in the selection of their words, and the use of language in writing, and have commanding personalities when they are allowed to develop properly, and well-developed dramatic faculties. Such persons are usually affable among their peers, with perhaps a slight tendency to be impatient with those who do not aspire to rise, or who may be classed in their subconscious minds as the lowly serfs of a past kingdom.

These persons can always be reached and appealed to through suggestions of sumptuousness and magnificence, and whatever may be honorable. They will succeed best in business matters wherein they may be managers, directors, controllers, or overseers, mayors, governors, or any high governmental officers, or holders of important positions in the courts of law. In more humble positions they will succeed as sheriffs, magistrates of small courts, or executive positions of a similar nature.

They have an excellent preparation and faculty for the study of law, and in an artistic manner they are fond of metals and working in metals, not as jewelers, but as designers and creators of beautiful and magnificent things of metal. As second choice, they would succeed as designers and creators of magnificent buildings or arrangers of beautiful homes, or the creators of beautiful costumes, and articles of adornment.

The physical weakness which they have inherited in this life are affections of the heart and brain, perhaps through overwork mentally, and tendencies toward weakness of the eyes, and toward fevers. They will find joy and recollection of familiar things from the past in traveling in such countries as Chaldea, Phoenicia, Italy, Sicily, Switzerland, and Scotland.

Polarity A
March 22 to April 17

Persons born in the first half of Period No. 1 will be more active in fighting their way to the top of the ladder of their ambitions than those in the B polarity. They will use all of their vital energy and power, and every physical means to achieve leadership and dominating positions, and they will be like warriors in mastering and controlling any situation or any line of work with which they are connected. Their constitutions will be fiery and strong, and their personal magnetism well developed, with excellent speaking voices and commanding style in writing.

Polarity B
April 17 to May 12

Those born in the last half of Period No. 1 will have greater tendencies to seek the goals of their ambitions in the fine arts or in the more refined and delicate places of life. They will be more genteel than those in the A polarity, if given the opportunity to develop their inherent tendencies, and they will be more subtle, more smiling, and more quiet in their achievements of success than those in the A polarity. Nevertheless, there is the same determination, with an additional characteristic that some may call *bull-headedness*. These persons will be found associated with art, drama, and music, either as hobbies or as professions if they have the opportunities to allow their natural tendencies to guide them.

PERIOD NO. 2
May 12 to July 3

Persons born in this period come into this life carrying from the Cosmic and from their last previous incarnations memories of many peculiar experiences and tendencies, characteristics, that make strange combinations. In the first place, they bring into this life from the past a deep-seated desire to travel and move about, or they have been successful and happy in this in a previous life. The continuation in this life in any one place or in any one line of thought, or in any one hobby for a long time spells monotony to these persons, and however they may try outwardly to associate themselves permanently with some place or set of conditions, the inner restlessness causes them to feel uncomfortable and to seek a change. In one of their incarnations they have been not only experienced in journeying, but in exploring, investigating, and in trying to taste all phases of life.

Everything that they associate themselves with is of the more delicate, refined, and temperamental nature. They have inherent desires to be well-mannered, thereby expressing tender natures, and the wish to be well-received and well-considered. There is a cosmic desire to search for novelties and the passing pleasures of human life that are wholesome, and yet filled with joy and happiness. Yet there is another equally strong desire, carried over from an old incarnation by each of these persons, to delve occasionally into the sciences and the more practical things of life, and these two desires constitute the strange complex that occasionally manifests itself in the lives of these persons.

They are practical, saving, conservative in many ways, and yet their lives are of the present hour always, and they have a tendency to let the future take care of itself because of their faith in the just reward that will come. They prefer to live free of the cares of this life, seeking peace and quiet whenever they are troubled; they are not easily led into quarrels, arguments, or disagreements. They love to spend much time in meditation. In many affairs there is a tendency to be fickle, or we may say that those judging them outwardly would believe this to be so, whereas in truth it is only another form of the expression of the desire for change and for new experiences.

They are honest, careful, ethically precise in many ways, and clean and wholesome in character, but are very apt to be misjudged because of their changeable natures. These persons must guard against being led into the company of those who seek only the pleasures of the flesh, for once they are started on a downward path, they become heavy drinkers, and are beggarly, careless, and given to disregard the niceties of life.

In the trades and professions, these persons will succeed well as traveling representatives, or persons connected with business affairs that require changes of location, changes of contact, with many branches, and fluctuating interests. There are inherent faculties and abilities which will make them excellent secretaries, designers, artists, saleswomen or salesmen, actors or actresses, concert entertainers, newspaper reporters, or servants in fine homes. A peculiar tendency on the part of these persons is that of marrying persons who will bestow titles upon them or will bring changes of position into their lives. Very often the women marry men who look upon them and treat them as queens or as countesses, and pay continued adoration to them, whereas the men often marry women who are well-to-do, and who look upon their husbands as kings in the homes.

Inherited physical weaknesses give a tendency toward troubles with the bladder, and toward rheumatic diseases, colds, and coughs. Often these colds will manifest through disturbance in the stomach or in the feet or eyes. These persons will find joy and interest in traveling through such countries as Norway, Denmark, the Netherlands, and Belgium, where they will contact sights and conditions familiar to them from the past.

Polarity A

May 12 to June 8

Those born in the first half of Period No. 2 will have very quick intellects, and will be more apt to enter into businesses that permit them to use their minds and fingers rather than all of the muscles of their bodies. In other words, quick minds, quick tongues, and quick hands will serve them usually well, and they are very apt to be employed in two occupations or have two hobbies and interests at the same time, and to give the impression to others that they are almost dual in their manner of living and expressing themselves. They should do everything that is in their power to develop the intellectual and mental side of their lives, because of inherited mental faculties. Persons in this polarity will make themselves known by their intellectual pursuits and will be credited with excellent education and excellent training, even if they have not actually had them in any school or academy.

Polarity B

June 8 to July 3

Those born in the last half of Period No. 2 are generally outstanding characters in the intellectual world, for they continually associate themselves with those interests or industries that deal with education, the fine arts, or the law. Their intellectual capabilities are more reserved and must be discovered, and they usually manifest in excellent memories, fine appreciation of language, intuitive senses that enable them to foresee and prophesy or perhaps sense oncoming conditions before anyone else may think of them. They are somewhat more stable in their physical changes of location, although the love of travel and of change of residence causes them to move occasionally. They will vacillate more in their intellectual pursuits and in their reading and studying than in their physical environment, however. These persons are able to serve as secretaries or associates in business to a greater degree than those in any other period or polarity.

PERIOD NO. 3
July 4 to August 25

Persons born in this period carry from the past into this life the experiences of great struggles and achievement through determination and self-mastership. In other words, we have in this period those who are already potentially self-masters and masters of fate. And they have a strong constitution, a fiery, impetuous nature, and the will power and ability to accomplish against great odds, if there is sufficient motive and some encouragement.

In addition to this inner nature, which is a part of their soul consciousness, their births during this period have given them from the Cosmic other related faculties and abilities which will enable them to be bold, confident, invisible characters in the achievement of any great purpose. These persons will challenge any obstacles that may arise in their lives, even though outwardly they may not realize that they have been stirred to action or aroused to a fighting spirit by obstacles that others may have looked upon as insurmountable or perhaps insignificant according to their natures. In other words, this is the type of person who can be encouraged and led into action by presenting an obstacle to him, as being one that others have failed to overcome. Naturally these persons are lovers of contest, and seekers of honors in contests, not merely for the aggrandizement, but because of the mastership it will establish.

They are apt at times to be boastful of their abilities and in this thing demonstrate a weakness that must be overcome. They never hesitate to risk lives or limbs, or their best interests, to achieve anything that they believe was destined for them to master, whether it is in association with their own personal interests or not. Naturally these persons, if properly placed and properly trained, become great leaders in movements or employments calling for the use of strong will power, strong hands, and strong principles. If allowed to have their own choice in professions, they will most generally succeed as captains or officers in an army, or as leaders in great movements calling for strong, masterful leadership.

In more conservative positions they will succeed as surgeons or chemists, or even as carpenters and contractors. They have an inherited inclination and liking, brought over from the past, for the making of small things that are intricate and of a mechanical nature. Therefore, they often are inventive and are successful in such lines as watchmaking, electrical designing, or the making of small mechanical devices of a very important nature.

Their physical weaknesses may manifest in the tendency toward diseases of the blood, such as carbuncles, ringworm, eczema, sores of the skin, yellow jaundice, and similar conditions. There is also a tendency toward trouble from gallstones or burning fevers, and these persons should be very careful of their diet, for they are apt to eat highly seasoned foods and too much meat. We will find these persons attracted to and interested in such places as Lombardy, Bavaria, northern France, and Paris, for there they will recall conditions that seem familiar.

Polarity A
July 4 to July 31

Persons born in the first half of Period No. 3 are very apt to be adventuresome and to travel a great deal seeking adventure and the doing of things that call for the risking of life and limb, and they are, therefore, natural explorers and investigators. If unable to travel considerably, they will explore even in their own immediate country, and be known by their restless desires to delve into the mystery of conditions that baffle the conservative nature of a person who is not so ready to risk his life. These persons make good leaders of armies, or leaders of naval forces, and they are often associated with political or reform movements, for they love conquest and can carry an issue to victory. These persons often lead double lives in many ways, for they will have many interests and two outstanding occupations or methods of applying the faculties of their natures.

Polarity B
July 31 to August 24

Those born in the last half of Period No. 3 generally succeed in achieving the attainment of some position that places them at the head of some great organization, as in some high political office equivalent to that of a governor, mayor, judge, or president. They are naturally kingly and queenly by all of their instincts and habits, and they love pomp and ceremony, limelight, and adoration and approval of the public. They live their lives in keeping with these desires, and, therefore, carefully guard their weaknesses and those habits which might jeopardize the high positions they seek, or which they attain, for they learned this lesson in a previous life. In any occupation, whether on the stage, in literary work, in business, or in social affairs, the persons in this polarity are leaders or outstanding characters, and the mediocre positions in life will not satisfy them. Children born in this polarity should be given every form of education and training that will enable them to hold high positions with efficiency and with honor to themselves and their parents.

PERIOD NO. 4
August 25 to October 15

Persons born in this period carry into this life from a previous incarnation the attainment of high personal powers, the positions of leadership that have to do with education, the fine arts, and especially the development of civilization, and the best interests of the public. Together with these characteristics, such persons have received from the Cosmic the additional benefits of wonderful faculties for study, and the attainment of knowledge, and the ability to express themselves in words or writing together with very fine memories, the ability to reason logically, and to live a life of estheticism if the opportunity is afforded.

These persons are hard to become acquainted with objectively, for their intellectual abilities and knowledge enable them to clothe themselves with the colors of their environment and to meet persons on their own level. We may find these persons in the most humble positions of life, seemingly occupied with pursuits and affairs of a lowly type, and yet we will discover through acquaintanceship that they are truly prepared and trained for higher and better positions then those in which we find them. On the other hand, we may find these persons in the highest positions of the literary world, or at the head of educational institutions where they give more thought to the advancement of humanity than to their own advancement.

The cosmic rhythm has created in them a natural desire for learning and for research, and they are very fond of mysteries, whether in fiction or in actuality. These persons also have the tendency to appreciate the power of words and the fine points in law and scientific knowledge. There is a tendency toward searching into the occult and into the secret and arcane wisdom of all ages, as well as into philosophy and religion, but in the latter sense the tendency is toward nonsectarianism and the building up of universal brotherhood and love.

These persons are very capable in trade or business, and make excellent merchants because of their ability to read human nature and to understand the desires and wishes of others. For that reason they would make good salesmen or saleswomen, or good instructors of sales forces, or writers and preparers of advertising and sales literature. Their ability to reason logically and to express their ideas with logical arguments makes them qualified for many positions where this natural ability can be used. Very often their abilities lead them into politics, where they succeed well, but not to the same extent that they would in some truly humanitarian profession.

These persons have usually acquired considerable advancement in metaphysical and occult illumination in a previous incarnation, and very often they were formerly adepts in one of the arcane brotherhoods, most often the Rosicrucian Order. There is something about their soul personality development and spiritual attainment that makes them truly great masters inwardly, and they are restless and unhappy until they contact in this incarnation that place or point in their soul progress where they left off in the last incarnation.

These persons should be guided to the Rosicrucian work or some similar course of study and development at an early age, for that will be the beginning of another phase of rapid progress and development for them. Honor, temperance, and mystical idealism, accompanied by an unusually wonderful imagination, are the keynotes of their real inner characters. We find these persons very often occupied in the present incarnation as literary workers, mathematicians, secretaries, writers, sculptors, poets, orators, school teachers, college professors, bankers, clergymen, or ambassadors.

The physical weaknesses, which are subtle physical tendencies of their natures, generally express themselves in so-called vertigoes, dizziness of the head or brain fatigue, accompanied sometimes by a slight degree of stammering or imperfection of enunciation, due to the rapid thinking and the attempt at rapid expression of thought. There may also be a tendency toward hoarseness, dry cough, or colds in the head. These persons will find great joy and happiness in visiting or traveling through such places as Flanders, Egypt, India, and most of all, the southern part of France.

Polarity A
August 25 to September 20

Persons born in the first half of Period No. 4 are generally shining lights in the educational and intellectual world. More women than men come into this period and become teachers of music, fine arts, or in a more humble way creators of costumes or workers at fine sewing and other trades or arts requiring nimbleness of finger and hand. On the other hand, the men of this period have a natural tendency toward the spiritual things of life, and would be excellent clergymen or teachers of ethics, philosophy, and morals, if they could express themselves freely and *outside of the limitations of sectarianism.* Persons in this polarity are generally very genial, good-natured, polished, cultured, and artistically and musically inclined. But this polarity also gives great strength of character and a dominating magnetism that would make them well qualified as physicians and surgeons, or judges and magistrates.

Children born in this polarity must be directed very carefully, because the imagination is highly developed and this may create in them imaginary ideas which they will represent as truth and thus fall into the habit of making false statements. They, too, much be guarded against a restlessness of nature, ever seeking the strange and peculiar things of life and ignoring the practical. Overstudy on the part of such children must be guarded against, because the nervous and mental systems will not stand the strain during childhood and early youth.

Polarity B
September 20 to October 15

Persons born in the last half of Period No. 4 are particularly well adapted to the use of their mental abilities and logical reasoning in making decisions and in coming to reasonable conclusions. They are well balanced in all of their faculties and have a great desire to balance all their thoughts and all their knowledge. In examining the evidence or the statements on any subject, or in any matter of dispute, they are sure to seek for the balance and to want to establish an equality in all things. The tendency in their lives is to be more or less esthetic, with a great love for the pretty, beautiful, luxurious, nice, and comfortable things of life. They are generally supporters or patrons of the arts and music, as well as drama, and make good artists and writers, especially of happy and fantastic tales with good moral principles involved. These persons are seldom ruffled or upset, and go through life with a tranquility and evenness that is a great help to others as well as themselves. They, therefore, should occupy such positions as enable them to hold conditions in certain bounds, or to direct the lives of children and young people along the lines of peace, harmony, and beauty.

PERIOD NO. 5
October 16 to December 6

Persons born in this period are generally those who attain great success and fame in their particular callings, although this success may not always be measured in worldly things or in a financial way. These persons carry over from the past incarnation one lesson which they have learned well, and which becomes the keynote of their inner, secret natures, and that is, that as one *gives and does for others,* so one attains and succeeds in life. Therefore, these persons are fundamentally generous, good-natured, kindly, and often free in their actions and lives to such an extent that their own success and progress seems to be nil from a material point of view, and for this reason they are often misjudged as failures in life.

On the other hand, they do acquire an unusual amount of knowledge, a great deal of culture and polish, an extreme amount of happiness and pleasure, and withal are comfortable and satisfied with their lot in life, even though it may be in poor circumstances or in humble position. In every crisis the Cosmic comes to their rescue and brings about satisfactory conditions. This, however, does not prevent them from seeking greater things and a greater abundance of this life's blessings. But they are philosophically inclined through the lessons they have learned in the past, and believe that they should give thanks every morning for life itself, and not complain if they have the least of the worldly blessings, for they realize that they have in their knowledge and in their mystical powers a greater asset than most other human beings, and for this they are eternally thankful.

These persons also bring into this life from the Cosmic, through the vibrations of the period in which they were born, an unusually philosophical nature, accompanied with the ability to acquire languages and to understand the spiritual and natural laws of the universe to an unusual degree. This makes it simple for them to acquire and master the principle of harmony in art, music, writing, and even in chemistry.

Being capable, therefore, of expressing themselves in so many different ways, these persons are really in possession of more hobbies throughout life than those born in any other period. Whenever they seek relaxation or a change from occupation, they can turn their hands to music, to mechanics, to art, or to the sciences, and dabble in any one of these things to a degree that almost borders upon professional expertness. For this reason they may enter into various occupations in their youth and change often as they go through life. They finally settle into positions where their complex abilities can be used, one by one, throughout the weeks and months, and thereby hold unique positions which other persons could not fill.

Fundamentally, there is a great love for animals, for outdoor sports, and for nature itself. They are open, frank, honest, and cheerful, and deplore deceit and underhandedness. They have carried over with them a very high degree of mystical development and of religious and spiritual attunement, and are often thrown into deep spells of spiritual meditation that others may look upon as despondency. They seem to sense the sufferings of the world as well as the pleasures of the world.

These persons would make excellent directors of organizations, where they are concerned with the scope of larger plans and things of a national or international importance rather than with the smaller details of executive management. They are capable of planning great schemes and carrying them out successfully, and for this reason they may enter the profession of advertisement writing and planning, sales organization work, or the control and management of schools, colleges, and universities. In business methods, however, their generosity, charity, and liberal nature does not bring them personal fortune, nor help to build up the financial end of their plans, but it does bring success in every other direction, which eventually leads to financial success. We are more apt to find these persons in the positions of judges, senators, lawyers, priests, doctors of law, professors in universities, newspaper editors, or magazine editors, or conductors of shops or places of antiques, or dealers in the arcane and mystical things of life.

In physical weaknesses the most common manifestation is in connection with inflammation of various parts of the body though colds or overwork, accompanied by conditions of the blood due to overeating or irregular eating, or the eating of rich foods. Skin diseases, rheumatic conditions, quinsy, and apoplexy are general conditions found with these people. These persons will find great joy and happiness in journeying through or visiting Babylon, Persia, Egypt, Palestine, and the strange byways of the Orient where they may come in contact with ancient familiarities, especially in Egypt, China, and Japan.

Polarity A
October 16 to November 11

Persons born in the first half of Period No. 5 are very aggressive in their business affairs because they have a nature that is filled with determination and energy. They do not rise to heights in the same channels as those in the B polarity, because those in the A polarity have a feeling that they must fight their way through life and must be everlastingly at something in order to keep themselves from slipping back into a mediocre position. The aggressiveness of the persons in this polarity leads them into many unique positions and makes them outstanding characters in their ability to accomplish difficult things. They have a tendency, however, toward accidents and toward delays through their own rash exertions. These persons will find themselves best fitted for positions in connection with the government, or as attorneys, occupied daily in arguments and dissensions, fighting for certain principles with considerable success.

Polarity B
November 11 to December 6

Those born in the last half of Period No. 5 are almost the opposite of those born in the A polarity in regard to aggressiveness. The warlike spirit of their nature is greatly subdued and they would rather stay away from a quarrel or argument than take any part in it. They believe that everything will eventually adjust itself successfully and properly without contention. They are more happy, cheerful, and free in their living than those in the A polarity, and while not seeking positions or labors or problems that call for strenuous physical effort, they do love to tackle problems that call for mystical understanding or intellectual mastership, and careful, logical reasoning for a solution.

These persons make very dependable friends, are often leaders of humanitarian movements, and occupy themselves more in helping others than in helping themselves. They enjoy the nice things of life, but always have an inclination to seek places that are covered, secret, or out of the way, and to associate with the persons who are of lowly or humble station and try to help them. On the other hand, these persons live an open, noble life, and constantly try to rise to greatest of mystical heights and become spiritually attuned with the highest forces in the universe. Great masters, great adepts, and those ready for the highest forms of mystical initiation are generally found in this polarity.

PERIOD NO. 6
December 7 to January 27

Those persons born in this period bring with them from the past incarnation a benediction which they have earned through suffering and much trial and pain. This benediction is in the form of a reward, and brings to these persons that happiness, joy, and indulgence in the pleasant things of life which they have not had before, but which they may have had an opportunity to enjoy, but discarded or cast aside in some previous incarnation, and then had to do without for a long time to learn the great lesson. However, being born in this period brings the benediction and blessing of attainment, peace, and attunement with the pleasant, cheerful, lovely things of human life.

As they use these pleasures, however, in this incarnation, so will they determine for themselves what their fate will be in their next incarnation. If they abuse the benediction that is theirs this time or cast it lightly aside in any way, it will be denied to them at the close of this incarnation and in a future one. To carry out this benediction, the cosmic vibrations of this period have given them certain faculties and functions which, if developed and applied properly, will bring them the joy and happiness they should have. Therefore, these persons have a natural tendency toward music, toward merriment, amusements, singing, pleasant voice, pleasing disposition, and a cheerful aspect of life.

There is a distaste born in them in this incarnation for anything sordid or deceitful, and virtue and honor are constant urges of their present, inner dispositions. For this reason, these people are not usually given to quarrelling or wrangling, nor to viciousness of any kind. Early in childhood and all through life they will show a tendency toward cleanliness in health, cleanliness in habits, and even a conservative attitude toward all indulgences. This makes many of the persons born in this period of the esthetic type, and we may easily recognize most of them by their physical appearance, for they seem to be of the mental temperament, and what one would casually call the artistic or musical type.

Seldom are they of very robust build or even of really robust health. Naturally, they tend to become musicians, artists, sculptors, actors, actresses, designers, or teachers of these arts and professions. The men make excellent jewelers, when they are not engaged in music, art, or drama, or dealers in silks and fine dress materials, embroideries, and things of this kind; for while they may go into these lines of business for the money there is in them, the real instinctive reason is their desire to be with and around fine materials and artistic creations. For the same reason they may go into the business of manufacturing and selling perfumes, or works of art, and become engravers or dealers in commodities that are for personal adornment or the decoration of homes.

These characters are ones which need sympathy and understanding if one is to become well acquainted with them, and they should never be forced to go into lines of business that deal with mechanics or heavy machinery, or coarse and muscular occupations. They are easily frightened and easily annoyed, and should never be placed as children or young people where there is great disturbance and a lack of quiet and peace. For such persons to be driven into war or into the melee of Wall Street or conditions of this kind is to be forced into an early annihilation of their best faculties and abilities, and to bring about a gradual breaking down of the body leading to early transition. These persons are really the makers of the mirth in life, and are usually the wholesome, sweet characters that we love to idealize.

In physical weaknesses, they generally suffer from nervousness due to overstudy or unpleasant environment, or very often from the suppression of natural functions due to an extreme moral viewpoint. In fact, this moral viewpoint may lead some of them to refrain from marriage until late in life, and in this repression they bring about a weakening of the constitution. Most of their physical suffering will be in parts of the body located in the abdomen, and especially in the bladder, kidneys, and bowels. These persons will find great joy and happiness in traveling through or visiting Arabia, parts of Austria, especially around Vienna, along the Mediterranean coast, and England and the New England states of America.

Polarity A
December 7 to January 2

Persons born in the first half of Period No. 6 are a little more serious in life than those in Polarity B, for they generally have a tendency to want to teach and promulgate their esthetic ideas and to help establish these things in their own community or nation. For this reason they may become associated with reform movements, or with educational movements, promulgating philosophy and ethics. Very often these persons become critics of the drama or of art and music, for it is their desire to separate the bad from the best in life. Even in all that seems perfect to others they see flaws, and can constructively and helpfully analyze and point out the errors that others do not see.

For this reason we find these persons in this polarity occupying very definite positions, generally as critics or teachers of a distinct class or even as judges in competitions, or as readers for magazines and newspapers, where they may pass judgment upon matter that is submitted for use. Their analytical minds enable them to accomplish a great deal of good for humanity, and especially in all of the arts and sciences, where they are more successful as analytical experts than as real developers of any one of the principles involved in any of the sciences and arts.

Polarity B
January 2 to January 27

Persons born in the last half of Period No. 6 are critical to an extreme extent, and while they do not allow this criticism to be applied for the benefit of others (for they hesitate to become known as reformers or to be identified with the criticism of matters of any kind), they nevertheless become critical of their own lives and of their own actions. This causes them considerable unrest and often makes them of that type which we call *Aquarian.* In other words, they often find themselves changing their opinions and doing things hastily and impulsively because of a sudden impression or a sudden critical attitude, and after the act is completed or the words spoken, they again analyze and criticize their actions and wonder why they did or said the things that have passed.

These persons also become antiquarians and love to delve into old bookshops, museums, and places of research, for they find pleasure and happiness in analyzing and criticizing, examining and studying the unusual things of life.

They make wonderful friends and are good entertainers, for they can talk well and long of unusual experiences and things which they have witnessed or enjoyed in life. There is the ability to build up stories and fictitious pictures and situations which enable them to become excellent writers of plays, dramas, or scenarios.

These persons enjoy life in a peculiar way through indulgence in their own unique forms of pleasure, and are often looked upon as being Bohemian, queer, or unusual in life. They are never accused, however, of being peculiar in their mental equipment, or of being irrational in any sense. They are always greatly loved by a large number of friends, and in all parties, entertainments, and associations are far from being *wallflowers,* or undesirable elements. These persons often attract to themselves an excellent companion for life in either marriage or business, and are really one of the important types making up the complex nature of humanity.

PERIOD NO. 7
January 28 to March 21

Those born in this period carry from their previous lives into this one the necessity for accomplishing very serious and important work in connection with the evolution of humanity. They are those who have brought into their lives through their own actions in the last incarnation, the need for learning, first, the serious aspects of life and, second, teaching these things to others through their own living or through their instruction.

They are usually those who have gone through a great many incarnations and are highly evolved and experienced in the lessons to be learned from all the experiences that life has to give in many foreign lands. For this reason, early in life these persons as children, or even as little babics, would be called *old souls,* and considered older than their years. From the Cosmic they have also inherited as a gift the ability to recall much of their past instruction, and most of the experiences they have had in life along with the additional faculty to systematize their knowledge and to acquire readily new knowledge and relate it to that which they have already stored up in the inner consciousness.

Therefore, it is not surprising to find that these persons in this period have an unusually deep imagination that seems to be prophetic and capable of imagining things which occurred in great antiquity, or which will occur in the future. They also have the ability to argue, to explain logically, and to present their thoughts and pictures systematically. They are, however, reserved in their utterances and reserved and dignified in all of their actions. They give one the feeling constantly of a person who feels that he or she is being observed and watched and analyzed, and, therefore, must be on guard in connection with every thought and act.

In judgment, they are severe because they are strict and careful. Unlike those in the fifth period, they do not allow their hearts to influence their judgments. To these persons *the law is the law,* and is both merciful and just, and no exceptions and no variations of the law must be allowed because of sentiment. Therefore, being stern and just they are generally greatly honored and respected, and seldom accused of being too severe or unfairly strict.

These persons believe that the great things of life are attained through study, and the careful building up of acquisitions along definite lines. They are extremely systematic, and take advantage of every principle of natural law and of man-made laws to assure themselves of the things they want in life and to protect what they have. They are not mercenary, but on the other hand they are not overly generous. They are, of course, naturally honest and more severe in regard to the exactness of statement and precision of things than those in any of the other periods. For all these reasons, these persons would make excellent judges, magistrates, or heads of large corporations and big business propositions.

A peculiar thing, however, is that in moderate circumstances and when born in mediocre positions, they often become employed in connection with such lines as plumbing, bricklaying, plastering, building, gardening, dyeing of cloth, printing, or in one of the other trades or businesses that are usually united in unions or under define wage scales as labor-trades. If these persons only knew that their inherent desire for exactness, precision, and truthfulness could lead them into higher occupations, such as magistrates and judges, they would seek education and training for such positions early in life and succeed well indeed.

On the other hand, their firm belief that the benefits of life and the necessities can be acquired only by slow acquisition and the careful attainment of them leads them into occupations that are well established, protected by union laws and government laws, and which seldom fluctuate in hours of employment or in salaries. Thus they hamper their own progress by a false understanding of the principles of life. Many of these persons also become nuns, monks, or members of monastic organizations or bodies, and live secluded lives where they can labor in their definite systematic manner to bring into their lives that which they feel is right.

The diseases which are natural to them through the vibrations of their period are impediments of the ears, teeth, or eyes, and sometimes of speech, and such conditions as proceed from colds, such as tuberculosis, and often pneumonia. On the other hand, their excellent constitutions enable them to live to a very old age, and they suffer only from jaundice or dropsy, with occasionally a touch of palsy or apoplexy. These persons are not usually ill until late in life, and are able to fight off many of the ailments that come to others. They will find great joy and pleasure in visiting such countries as Turkey, the Balkan states, Spain, parts of Africa, and South America.

Polarity A
January 28 to February 23

Persons born in the first half of Period No. 7 are very often led into occupations that are unusual, such as those of chemical experts, criminologists, investigators, explorers, research workers in ancient history, archeology, geology, and similar subjects. They are easily classified as being profound in knowledge, and devoted to only one, or possibly two, subjects in life. They usually dress in a quiet manner and give the appearance of being much older than they are. They show extreme reserve, a tendency toward orthodox and religious devotion, caring little for the gaieties of life, and seldom patronizing anything that is frivolous or transitory.

They are diligent workers, consistent, dependable, careful, and often employed in the same positions or same lines of work throughout their entire lives. These persons are often known as the *salt of the earth*, and are wonderful friends to those who can make a contact beneath the surface and win their favor. There is a desire to reform the world in certain regards, but these persons are consistent enough to adopt the reform themselves and live the life and set an example.

Polarity B
February 23 to March 21

Persons born in the last half of Period No. 7 are quite opposite to those of Polarity A, inasmuch as they are not quite so serious in life and do seek some pleasure and happiness as a relaxation and reaction from their more serious studies and occupations. The persons in this polarity have an unusual tendency toward mysticism, occultism, and the mysterious things of the universe, and of nature. The persons in this polarity seem to acquire more fortune in a material sense than those in Polarity A, and often attain considerable fame in their particular fields of effort.

However, they are quite dual in nature, and are capable of living a dual life inasmuch as they may be outwardly at the head of a great organization, or contacting the public in a smiling, happy mood, while at home or in the privacy of their own seclusion they may be quiet, reserved, and more interested in the deep, more serious things of life than one would suspect. These persons have a great magnetic power, which they can exert easily over others, and have a tendency to read easily the minds of other persons and to project their consciousness into space and there sense the thoughts and actions of others. These persons also love to be near the water and love to take long journeys, more for the purpose of studying human nature or studying the history and conditions of the country and place than for pleasure, although they do enjoy being on the water and in cities near it.

SELF-MASTERY AND FATE

CHAPTER 17

THE CYCLES OF REINCARNATION

JUST as each year of our lives begins a new cycle, and each one of these cycles is divided into periods of progression and development, with intermittent periods of action and reaction, and just as the general cycle of life is divided into periods of seven years through which we progress from a purely physical creature to a more or less perfected spiritual being, merely clothed in a physical body, so our whole existence in this universe is divided into larger periods of approximately 144 years which constitute the periods in a long cycle of incarnation and reincarnation.

Just as you who read this book today may be in the sixth period of your complex life cycle in this incarnation, and in the fourth period of your yearly cycle, so you may be in the eighth or the tenth or the fiftieth or one hundredth period of your long cycle of reincarnations.

Whether one believes in the doctrines of evolution of the species of man or not, there is one thing quite sure, and that is that man as a definite and distinct species has been evolving since the time he became man as a distinct creature. In other words, man as MAN had some beginning, whether that beginning was spontaneous, as the orthodoxy of some religions claim, or whether man's beginning was the culmination of stages of evolution preceding his distinct nature. Therefore, from the time of the beginning of man as the highest creature in God's Kingdom, man has continued to evolve as a man, and this evolution will continue forever.

We may liken the beginning of man's career to the making of a book. The critical materialist may say that a book with its beautiful binding, well-printed pages, attractive illustrations, gold lettering, and gilded edges, was nothing more or less at one time than a mass of cotton pulp, silkworm strands, and mineral crystals. He may say truthfully that the book we now admire evolved beautifully out of lesser things, and, therefore, had a very primitive beginning in the elements of the earth, plant, and animal life. But the mystic or the philosopher might reply and say that the book never was a book until all of these elements had been gathered together by a master mind, their natures changed, their tendencies altered, and new combinations created, and in the twinkling of an eye brought together spontaneously into a new thing called a BOOK, and that preceding its creation as a book, it did not exist even in any primitive form.

Thus the mystic is not concerned with what changes the evolution of earthly elements may have brought into the process of preparation for the physical composition of man's body, but is concerned primarily with the creation of man by the placing of the highest consciousness of God within a physical form and thereby spontaneously creating and bringing into existence a new species, a new creature, a new manifestation of Godliness called *man*. From the time of man's creation onward, the physical evolution that occurs in his body is purely secondary to the greater evolution that is occurring in his spiritual nature and in his soul personality.

It is unquestionably true that man's physical form today is a vast improvement over the form that primitive man possessed. Unquestionably the physical form of man has evolved from a lower type of man's body to a higher type of man's body, and such evolution has not reached its heights nor even sensed its ultimate goal. Man is as responsible for this physical evolution as is God, for as man re-creates his environment, it reacts upon his physical as well as his mental development, and perfects the upward tendency of his evolution on Earth.

The evolution of a person's soul personality proceeds through its contact with the experiences, trials, tribulations, and lessons of this earthly life as well as through its contact with the universal, Divine Consciousness of the Cosmic Mind of God.

The mystics of all lands and the devout students of religion of all lands—which means more than three fourths of the Earth's population—realize that the spiritual evolution and perfection of man could not occur in the short period of one incarnation. That would be equivalent to but one period of seven years in the earthly life cycle of each person here on Earth. If we look upon the earthly life cycle and realize that each seven years brings its progress and increasing evolution to the soul personality and mind, as well as to the body of each individual on this earthly plane, we will realize how different it would be if each of us lived but one period of that cycle, for instance, from our birthday to our seventh year.

Certain wonderful changes and improvements in the body, mind, and soul personality would unquestionably take place in that short span of existence, but look at the remarkable changes that occur in the next period, from the seventh to the fourteenth birthday, and then again from the fourteenth to the twenty-first, and so on.

If we think of the evolution and cycle of the soul personality and of the existence here on Earth in a physical body as being like the periods of a life cycle, we will see that each incarnation in a physical body is like a period of seven years in the earthly cycle. It is only through progressive experiences and the continuation of experiences that we can evolve. If there were but one period in which we lived on Earth, and if that period were even 300, 400, or 500 years long, it would not be sufficient for each soul personality to learn all that it must learn, to suffer all that it must suffer, to master all that it should master, and attain all that is attainable in order to reach that degree of perfection which would constitute a reason for our existence at all.

How often we notice a young man or young woman of brilliant mind and of unusual capabilities, and ask the question, how old is he? or, how old is she? We want to know whether these young persons are in the second or third period of their earthly life cycle. In other words, we want to know whether they are in the period between seven and fourteen, or fourteen and twenty-one. This is to enable us to comprehend the reason for the extraordinary mental development or spiritual progress that we notice in these children. Is it not just as appropriate, then, when we find a person highly evolved in spiritual things, well developed in the mastership over earthly conditions and greatly illumined in the mystical and natural laws of the universe, to ask, in what incarnation this person may be? We mean, to ask whether this person is in the third, fourth, twentieth, fiftieth, or one hundredth period of incarnation on this earth plane. We have no way of answering such questions, but still we ask them and wonder about it. We often notice in young people that look, that poise, that character, that something that warrants us in saying, "It is an old soul." Whence came this universal feeling that some have lived much longer than others?

This is not a plea in behalf of the doctrine of reincarnation, for the doctrine itself needs no plea at my hands, and this is not the place in which to present an outline of the doctrine, or submit any of a thousand or more arguments which substantiate the doctrine. My sole intention here is to arouse questions in your mind and start some very interesting thinking that may lead you to some worthwhile conclusions.

A few years ago the mere mention of any idea connected with the belief in reincarnation elicited smiles and facetious comments. Today, clergymen of many denominations and leaders in their respective fields of work, eminent writers, philosophers, editors, physicians, and scientists freely comment on their belief in the doctrine of reincarnation and point out the fact that it is the only merciful, just, logical, sane, and rational explanation of the differences we see in life, and of the inequalities, the tests, trials, and joys and blessings enjoyed so differently by all human beings.

The doctrine was once a fundamental principle in the Christian religion, but was arbitrarily rejected by those who could not comprehend it, and today the Christian religion is the only one in which the doctrine is completely set aside and misunderstood. Fortunately, the great leaders in the Christian church are reviving the doctrine again through a gradual comprehension of its real principles and of its truth.

The important point I wish to impress upon your mind is that the doctrine of reincarnation presents to us the one dominating and overtone cycle of life by which all other cycles are standardized, and from which all other undulating periods emanate. Without a comprehension of the cycle of incarnations, all other cycles are incomprehensible, and one may say that without a comprehension of the true nature of our ontological existence, all other details of our earthly life or of our spiritual existence in the universe are likewise incomprehensible.

Let him who reads this book, therefore, find it within his heart or within the scope of his rational thinking to lay aside bias and prejudice and come out of the darkness of unbelief or wrong belief, and look into the greater truths that are offered by the mystic and the student of the true spiritual laws. Read such books as will give you a better understanding of your true relationship to the universe, to God, and to humanity. Discover your own place in the life you are living and in the lives of all other beings. Learn the powers that you possess and thereby break through the fictitious wall of limitations that has been placed about you by man-made creeds and modern doctrines. Expand your consciousness until you become attuned with the infinite, where all truths, laws, and principles will appeal to the rationalism of your soul and the wisdom of the Divine Mind within you. This will bring added degrees of mastership and of leadership.

Within you and about your own existence are the greatest fields for exploration that man has ever known. And while you are delving into the mysteries of your business, the mysteries of your social, financial, and other affairs, do not neglect to delve into the mysteries of your life, the mysteries of your own being. In other words, recall the ancient scriptural injunction: "With all thy getting, get understanding."

Important Notice

The publishers of this book wish to call the reader's attention to the fact that neither the editors, publishers, nor the author of the book can undertake to work out the personal cycles or the individual periods relating to any personal or business problems which may confront any reader of this book. The system set forth in this book has been tried and tested for many years before it was issued in this form, and the instructions contained in it are sufficient to enable any man or woman gradually to apply the system successfully and to gain the utmost benefit through such application.

The sale of this book does not carry with it, therefore, the privilege of personal correspondence and personal help in the matter of working out individual problems. While the publishers will appreciate comments and suggestions for the improvement of this book in its future editions, they will not be able to answer personal letters asking for help in connection with the problems of business, health, social, or other affairs of any individual.

Reference Indicator

The book *Self-Mastery and Fate with the Cycles of Life,* which thousands have read and used daily, proves what economists and scientists know—that there is a periodicity in human and natural events. In life there are fortunate and unfortunate hours for every act. We are pleased to introduce to the readers of this book a *simple indicator* based on the charts of the book which at a single glance reveals the hourly periods—accurately, mathematically true. One glance at this indicator informs the reader of the nature of the daily periods governing his life—no guesswork.

This handy reference indicator can be carried in the pocket. It is ever-ready to reveal the tendencies of the cycles affecting you. Accompanying it is a pamphlet that fully explains the things to avoid during certain periods, or the profitable periods that await you. Every reader of the above book should possess this practical indicator. If you do not have it, secure the reference indicator and pamphlet today. You can order it by going to our web site at: *www.rosicrucian.org* and clicking on STORE.

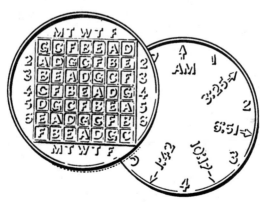

INDEX

A

Almanacs, 95
Anabolic phases, 90
Astro-phenomenon, 126

B

Birthday, 47,51,61,63-67,72,75,
    81,131,137-138,174
Book:
    Rosicrucian Principles
    for the Home and
    Business, 9
Brotherhood, 152-153

C

Calendar, 47-52;66,138
Catabolic phases, 90
Character, 13,40,43,46,69,125,
    128-133,138,146,148,151,
    153,154,159,161,162,175
Charts, 11-12,101-106,139
    A. Calendar for any year, 49
    B. Cycle No. 2 or No. 3, 50
    C. Moon's cycles, 93
    D. Seven periods of daily
       cycle, 103
    E. Periods for each day of
       the week, 105
    F. Periods and polarities of
       soul cycle, 139
Childbirth, 94,95
Cosmic, 11,13,16-20,25-27,
    30-34,41,42,45,55,56,61,
    66,72,73,110,113,125,127,
    129,131,133,135-136,141,
    144,145,151,152,156,160,173

Countries, regions, and cities:
    Africa, 167
    America, 9-10,12,45,162
    Arabia, 225
    Austria, 162
    Babylon, 158
    Balkan states, 167
    Bavaria, 150
    Belgium, 147
    Chaldea, 143
    China, 158
    Denmark, 147
    Egypt, 154,158
    England, 162
    Flanders, 154
    France, 150,154
    Greenwich, 98
    India, 154
    Italy, 143
    Japan, 158
    Lombardy, 150
    Mediterranean coast, 162
    Netherlands, 147
    New England, 162
    North America (See America)
    Norway, 147
    Orient, 22,158
    Palestine, 158
    Paris, 150
    Persia, 158
    Phoenicia,143
    Russia, 138
    Scotland, 143
    Sicily, 143
    South America, 167
    Spain, 167

Attorney, 159
Author, 9,140
Banker, 113,153
Broker, 65
Carpenter, 135,149
Chemist, 149
Clergymen, 58,153,175
Contractor, 149
Controller, 143
Corporation, head of, 10, 119,166
Costumes, creator of, 143, 154
Criminologist, 168
Designer, 143,146,149,161
Director, 10,71,121,143,157
Drama critic, 163
Editor, 158,175
Engraver, 57,161
Entertainer, 146,164
Expert, 132,163,168
Farmer, 187
Governor, 52,119,143,151
Inventor, 41
Investigator, 133,150,168
Labor, 94,122,159,166
Lawyer, 65,113,117,121, 122,158
Leader, 142,149,159,175,176
Lecturer, 56
Magistrate, 119,143,154,166
Manager, 143
Manufacturer, 36,65,68
Mathematician, 33,153
Mayor, 52,119,143,151
Mechanic, 157,162
Merchant, 58,152
Messenger, 57
Military, 69

Monk, 167
Musician, 65,134-136,161
Newspapermen, 70
Nun, 167
Officer, 64,66,207
Official, 52,58,67,113,117, 120,121
Orator, 153
Overseer, 143
Painter, 134
Palm reader, 128
Philosopher, 41,172,175
Physician, 58,65,154,175
Plasterer, 166
Poet, 153
Police authority, 119
Politics, 153
President, 10,151
Priest, 158
Professor, 153,158
Proprietor, 36
Psychiatrist, 41,88
Psychologist, 41,88
Publisher, 96
Referee, 61,73,119
Reformer, 163
Reporter, 57,146
Representative, 67,114,146
Sales force instructor, 152
Salesman, 22,56,114,116,118, 120,122,146,152
Saleswoman, 146,152
Scientist, 25,175
Sculptor, 153,161
Secretary, 146,148,153
Senator, 52,67,119,158
Serf, 142
Servant, 58,60,115,116,118, 120,121,146

THE ROSICRUCIAN ORDER
Purpose and Work of the Order

The Rosicrucian Order, AMORC, is a philosophical and initiatic tradition. As students progress in their studies, they are initiated into the next level or degree.

Rosicrucians are men and women around the world who study the laws of nature in order to live in harmony with them. Individuals study the Rosicrucian lessons in the privacy of their own homes on subjects such as the nature of the soul, developing inituition, classical Greek philosophy, energy centers in the body, and self-healing techniques.

The Rosicrucian tradition encourages each student to discover the wisdom, compassion, strength, and peace that already reside within each of us.

www.rosicrucian.org

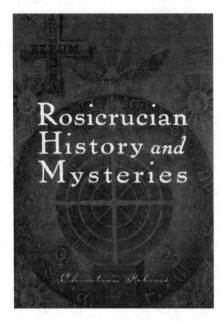

Rosicrucian History and Mysteries

by Rosicrucian author
Christian Rebisse

Softcover, 7.5 in. x 10.5 in.
244 pages

Suggested retail price: $24.95

The Rosicrucian Order, AMORC, is proud to announce the publication of this new work by Rosicrucian author Christian Rebisse. Originally published in French in 2003, this scholarly work is now available in English. This book is excellently researched—complete with endnotes, an index, a chronology, and a thematic bibliography suggesting sources for further reading. *Rosicrucian History and Mysteries* is abundantly illustrated with over 90 illustrations—many from rare and unusual sources. Here is the definitive history of Rosicrucianism, from the earliest of times to the present. This book is a must read for anyone interested in the Rosicrucian Order. Your Rosicrucian library will not be complete without this exceptional volume.

For other books published by the Rosicrucian Order, AMORC, please visit www.rosicrucian.org

Treasures of the Rosicrucian Egyptian Museum

A Catalogue

by *Lisa Schwappach-Shirriff, M.A.*
Curator
Rosicrucian Egyptian Museum

Softcover, 7.5 in. x 10.5 in.
160 pages; color

Suggested retail price: $24.95

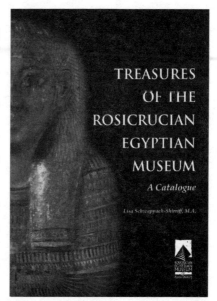

The history of the Rosicrucian Egyptian Museum in San Jose, California, began with a dream. H. Spencer Lewis, the leader of the museum's sponsoring organization, the Rosicrucian Order, AMORC, cherished this dream and through his efforts the museum came into being. Today, the Rosicrucian Egyptian Museum houses the largest collection of Egyptian, Assyrian, and Babylonian artifacts on exhibit in western North America.

This catalogue features the museum's major artifacts, including more than 250 artifact photos in color. Also included are essays providing fascinating insights into the daily life and culture of the ancient Egyptians, and a history of the Rosicrucian Egyptian Museum and its magnificent collection. With its captivating essays and beautiful photos, this museum catalogue brings ancient Egypt to life!

For other books published by the Rosicrucian Order, AMORC, please visit www.rosicrucian.org. *And for more information about the Rosicrucian Egyptian Museum, please visit* www.egyptianmuseum.org